Supply Chain Planning

Supply Chain Planning

Practical Frameworks for Superior Performance

Matthew J. Liberatore and Tan Miller

Supply Chain Planning: Practical Frameworks for Superior Performance
Copyright © Business Expert Press, 2012.

First published in 2012 by
Business Expert Press, LLC
222 East 46th Street, New York, NY 10017
www.businessexpertpress.com

ISBN-13: 978-1-60649-316-8 (paperback)

ISBN-13: 978-1-60649-317-5 (e-book)

DOI 10.4128/ 9781606493175

Business Expert Press Supply and Operations Management collection

Collection ISSN: 2156-8189 (print)
Collection ISSN: 2156-8200 (electronic)

Cover design by Jonathan Pennell
Interior design by Exeter Premedia Services Private Ltd.,
Chennai, India

First edition: 2012

10 9 8 7 6 5 4 3 2 1

Printed in the United States of America.

Abstract

In today's competitive global economy, a firm's market position and bottom-line financial performance is closely linked to its supply chain performance. All too often considerable managerial resources are directed toward planning activities and processes with little in the way of tangible results and outcomes. What supply chain executives require is the know-how to efficiently and effectively direct their planning activities so that the results lead to better business decisions from the long-term down to day-to-day operations. In this book, we present proven, practical management frameworks and techniques used by the authors to support supply chain operations management and planning in private industry. These frameworks describe supply chain strategic planning and project selection techniques, integrated manufacturing-distribution planning and scheduling approaches, performance measurement and balanced scorecard methodologies, customer logistics and inventory deployment decision support systems, and other well-tested management frameworks.

The book is intended for supply chain managers and executives in private industry and the public sector, as well as graduate and advanced undergraduate students. Practitioners will obtain valuable new insights and examples of implementable frameworks and methods for managing their supply chain functions and organizations. Students will develop an understanding of leading edge, real world approaches for supply chain strategic planning and scheduling, decision support, project development and selection, performance measurement and many other key activities.

Keywords

supply chain planning, supply chain frameworks, supply chain management, operations management, balanced scorecard, supply chain performance measurement, supply chain metrics, strategic planning, production planning and scheduling, logistics, decision support systems

Contents

Foreword

My first exposure to the discipline of supply chain management was in the fall of 1969 when, as an undergraduate business major at the University of Notre Dame, I took an elective course in *Physical Distribution Management*. It was certainly a more innocent time for logisticians, for the management objective in those days typically consisted of balancing a limited set of finished goods distribution costs against selected customer service goals, and almost always for domestic firms.

It seems axiomatic, almost to the point of trite, for supply chain management professionals to cite the daunting complexity of the challenges they routinely confront. Self-important puffery? Maybe 40 years ago but not today. Consider the overwhelming evidence: supply chains defined from supplier relationship management on one end to customer relationship management on the other, with all aspects of operations in between. Add the formidable challenges of worldwide sourcing and markets, attendant international finance (duties, taxes, exchange rates), strategic sourcing, rapid proliferation of product and service offerings with ever-declining life cycles, intense pressures to minimize capital and costs without sacrificing ever more stringent performance goals, risk mitigation, sustainability, the need for flexible and agile strategies and so on, and the lament seems more than reasonable.

So … how should one confront such challenges? One option is to waste energy with useless hand-wringing and plod along with little more than survival tactics. Another is to willingly embrace the complexity and confront it directly. However, without the proper strategies and analytical tools the latter quickly degrades into another exercise of management rah-rah devoid of results. Enter Messrs. Miller and Liberatore.

It has been my experience across a number of universities that a core course in operations management is often poorly taught, dreaded by students, and offers wholly inadequate coverage of supply chain management. Moreover, there are perhaps only a dozen or so first-rate supply chain management programs in the United States. This is depressing if not outright scandalous … and shows few signs of near-term improvement. The current text fills a major hole in the typical curriculum.

From the outset the authors admirably stress the importance of explicitly linking supply chain strategy to the larger corporate strategic goals and objectives. We are properly reminded of that crucial linkage at the outset of every chapter. They go on to describe in detail an organized, hierarchical, disciplined planning framework and process organized around the classic categories of strategic, tactical and operational decisions. The emphasis throughout is cross-functional, which is itself a refreshing departure from the outmoded silo management mentality that is still firmly embedded in many companies.

It is easy enough to leave a description of analytical frameworks and strategies in the abstract. One is then left with little more than empty prescriptions and platitudes. Not this time. Throughout the text the authors cogently describe specific approaches, tools and techniques that have been shown to deliver concrete results in practice. To that end they discuss in detail implementation examples from American Olean Tile Company and Pfizer/Warner Lambert. It is highly unusual for firms today to allow even their name to be associated with strategic approaches. Both firms are to be congratulated for their willingness to share their experiences in such an open environment.

I have spent the better part of 40 years developing and using various operations research-based tools to address strategic, tactical, and operational problems confronted by various government agencies and private sector firms. These experiences have repeatedly driven home the necessity of selecting technology consistent with the complexity of the problem, rather than opting for an expedient, oversimplified approach that necessarily fails in the end. Therefore, I was especially interested in the tools and techniques described and recommended by the authors. They do not disappoint. Once again, their emphasis on a hierarchical planning process is first rate. In particular, they demonstrate the need for complementary yet distinct tools for each level, and both commonality and granularity differences for the supporting databases. These are absolutely critical distinctions.

With respect to appropriate technology, I was especially gratified to see that not even once do the authors even mention, much less recommend, the use of the all-purpose, "analytical" solution to contemporary problems: the ubiquitous spreadsheet. It is a source of great personal frustration to witness the gross overuse of a tool which is essentially nothing more than high-speed arithmetic with eye-catching graphics. Rather, the authors argue persuasively for the use of truly advanced analytical approaches such as those employing mathematical optimization and stochastic simulation, those with the power required to successfully address the complex resource allocation problems that supply chain professionals must necessarily confront.

For those readers who remain skeptical, the authors persuasively prove their case by citing numerous examples of impressive savings achieved and costs avoided. They go on to emphasize that this is not a one-time event. Rather, the process, tools and expertise must be institutionalized in order to ensure a continuing stream of positive results.

It is clear that supply chain management complexity will continue to trend upward indefinitely. To confront it successfully requires diligent, long-term commitment to the most advanced analytical approaches available. Messrs. Miller and Liberatore show us the way forward in a way that none have previously achieved. We properly admire their achievement. It is up to the rest of us to follow their lead.

Dr. Jeffrey Karrenbauer
President of Insight Inc.
Manassas, Virginia

CHAPTER 1

Introduction

In today's competitive global economy, a firm's market position and bottom-line financial performance is closely linked to its supply chain performance. All too often considerable managerial resources are directed toward planning activities and processes with little in the way of tangible results and outcomes. What supply chain executives require is the know-how to efficiently and effectively direct their planning activities so that the results lead to better business decisions from the long-term down to day-to-day operations. In this book, we present proven, practical management frameworks and techniques used by the authors to support supply chain operations management and planning in private industry. These frameworks provide methodologies for organizing and managing critical activities such as supply chain strategic planning and project selection, integrated manufacturing and distribution planning, performance measurement, and customer logistics and inventory deployment, to name a few.

In this book, we illustrate how managers can and should employ planning frameworks to organize and manage all major supply chain functions and activities. While a firm clearly must have a framework to guide its overall supply chain strategic planning process, so too should the firm have a well-established planning framework for its individual supply chain functions such as transportation, manufacturing, and logistics. Further, and most critically, all these supply chain planning frameworks must support and align with the firm's overall business goals and objectives.

Objectives of the Book

In over twenty years of private industry experience, we have implemented numerous supply chain frameworks, decision support systems, and performance measurement systems to manage supply chain functions.

Our experience has taught us that firms which place strong emphasis on these approaches make themselves significantly more competitive and agile relative to firms that under invest in these areas.

We have several objectives in writing this book. First we wish to communicate to other supply chain practitioners and executives the importance of investing in the frameworks and systems that we describe. These methods have served us well in practice and we highly recommend these approaches. Secondly, all the methodologies and frameworks we present can readily be implemented. One objective of reviewing the numerous frameworks that will follow is to raise the visibility of these approaches and methods. A related objective is to describe these frameworks in easy to follow illustrations. We hope in doing so we will facilitate the implementation of these frameworks and methodologies by others who wish to utilize them.

Why Are Supply Chain Frameworks Critical to a Firm's Success

Firms that actively employ supply chain planning frameworks as a standard business practice give themselves a true competitive advantage. As we will demonstrate throughout the book, firms that embrace the methodologies and discipline fostered by a framework-based approach make themselves agile, and so are capable of effectively and rapidly responding to ever-changing business conditions. Leading edge characteristics of these firms include the ability to link and coordinate their planning activities and actions from the long-run, strategic horizon to the medium-term tactical and short-run operational horizons. The linkages between planning levels is hierarchical, meaning that plans developed at the strategic level guide and direct the tactical level, and plans developed at the tactical level guide and direct the operational level, so that all plans and actions are in alignment with the firm's high level strategy. This overarching hierarchical perspective provided by well implemented supply chain planning frameworks facilitates improved decision-making, higher customer service levels and improved operating efficiencies for firms. For example, later in this book, we review the case of a ceramic tile manufacturer that reduced its annual operating costs by approximately 10% and improved its customer service fill rates after implementing a hierarchical manufacturing and logistics planning framework.

We also detail the case of a large pharmaceutical and consumer health-care firm that invested heavily in hierarchical supply chain planning frameworks over many years. In particular, we examine how by utilizing its existing planning frameworks and related decision support systems, this firm responded rapidly and successfully to dramatically changing business conditions that created a significant stress on the firm's logistics capacity. This firm was able to maintain very high fill rates and avoid potential revenue losses of $20 million during a period of rapid business change. Another supply chain planning framework that we describe is that of a multibillion dollar confectionery division of a diversified con-sumer products and pharmaceutical firm. A key component of this firm's very broad hierarchical planning framework consisted of a global manu-facturing planning decision support system. We will review the strategic and tactical components of this system that identified over $5 million in potential annual operational savings.

The three examples just described offer a brief glimpse of the types of cases and supply chain planning frameworks which we present through-out this book. To set the stage for the remainder of this book, we now introduce two "linked" frameworks:

1. *A Business and Supply Chain Planning Framework, and*
2. *A Supply Chain Function Planning Framework.*

We will consider each of these frameworks separately, and then discuss the linkages and interdependencies which facilitate viewing these frame-works as one coordinated, unified firm-wide process.

A Business and Supply Chain Planning Framework

Figure 1.1 presents a simple framework depicting an integrated process where a firm's overall business goals and objectives define its supply chain organization's goals and objectives. Specifically, in its business strategic planning process, a company must address such key issues as overall corporate objectives, market share and profitability goals, and

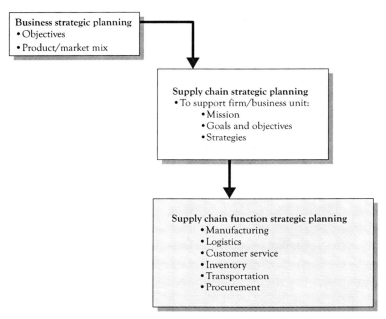

Figure 1.1. Integrated business and supply chain strategic planning framework.

business and product mix targets. Strategic planning decisions relating to overall corporate objectives then drive strategic supply chain plans and decisions. For example, market share and product mix objectives will strongly influence a firm's supply chain capacity and service strategies. Other high-level supply chain strategies are also developed at this stage to support business goals and objectives. Examples of such strategies would include setting targets for overall customer service levels and maximum inventory investment levels, and creating key customer strategic initiatives.

Once a firm's supply chain planning team has established its high-level strategies, the functions within this organization must then develop and implement their individual respective strategies. As Figure 1.1 depicts, functions such as manufacturing, logistics, and transportation each must plan their own strategies to support overall supply chain goals and objectives, and ultimately those of the business. For example, the manufacturing organization's plans must address such issues as planned production capacity levels for the next three years and beyond, the location and number of facilities its plans to operate, and so on. Other functions such as logistics, transportation, and procurement will face different but similarly critical issues and decisions. Later in the book we will review in greater detail what we describe here as an integrated business and supply chain planning framework. For now, however, as illustrated in Figure 1.1, this integrated strategic planning process consists of three components:

1. *Business Strategic Planning—which drives and guides*
2. *Supply Chain Strategic Planning—which drives and guides*
3. *Strategic Planning by Individual Supply Chain Functions.*

The distinction between steps 2 and 3 is as follows. In step 2, the senior leaders of the supply chain organization (i.e., the leaders of all the individual supply chain functions) collectively establish the high-level strategy for their organization. In step 3, each individual supply chain function (e.g., manufacturing) develops a strategic plan for its own organization. This individual plan naturally must support the overall supply chain plan generated in step 2.

To illustrate this integrated process, consider the following brief example. Let's assume that the business unit strategic planning process results in a decision that production capacity should be increased by 40% over the next five years to support planned sales growth (step 1). The supply chain strategic planning team receives this input, and its planning process (step 2) then determines that the firm will generate this capacity increase through internal expansion rather than using third party contract manufacturing. Plans developed at the overall supply chain level may be more specific—such as a general decision that capacity should be added specifically in Southeast Asia. The level of detail specified in step 2 will vary by firm. Next, in step 3 at the supply chain function level, the manufacturing group engages in its individual strategic planning process. At this level, manufacturing generates a detailed strategy addressing such issues as the specific location where it will build additional capacity, the technology planned for the facility, the targeted labor versus automation mix, and so on. Similarly, each other major supply chain function such as transportation will also conduct its strategic planning process in support of the overall supply chain strategic plan. This completes the three step integrated business and supply chain strategy planning framework.

We next introduce a framework for individual supply chain function planning. As we will discuss, at the supply chain function level, the planning process becomes much more detailed. To accommodate the granularity required at this level, each supply chain function must utilize a *hierarchical* planning framework which can address all issues ranging from the long run strategic to the very short run operational.

A Hierarchical Supply Chain Planning Framework

The planning activities and decisions that management must make for a supply chain function range from the extremely long run to the short run day to day. Further, the characteristics of these activities and decisions range from those requiring vast resources and managerial time (as measured by cost, required planning inputs, level of risk and other attributes) versus those requiring relatively minimal time and resources. For example, consider the vast differences in the required inputs for, and implications of, a plant location and sizing decision versus a one week production line scheduling decision. To effectively address this broad spectrum of management and operational control activities and decisions required in any major supply chain function (e.g., manufacturing), it is necessary to separate the future planning horizon into three buckets:

1. Strategic Planning,
2. Tactical Planning, and
3. Operational Planning

These three planning horizons must be closely and hierarchically linked to assure aligned decision-making, and we will discuss techniques and strategies to facilitate this alignment in Chapter 3. The interested reader is also referred to Appendix 1A to learn more about the rationale and process of hierarchical planning, as well as the types of decisions made at each level of the planning process.

A Generic Framework for Supply Chain Planning and Management

In this section, we link the business and supply chain planning framework and the hierarchical supply chain planning framework just reviewed to form a unified business and supply chain planning framework.

Figure 1.2 displays a generic business and supply chain planning framework. We describe this framework as *generic* because it illustrates how the planning activities of any individual supply chain function can (and should) be linked into the overall business and supply chain strategic planning process of an organization. Examples of significant individual supply chain functions would include, but are not limited to:

- Manufacturing
- Logistics
- Customer service
- Inventory
- Transportation
- Procurement

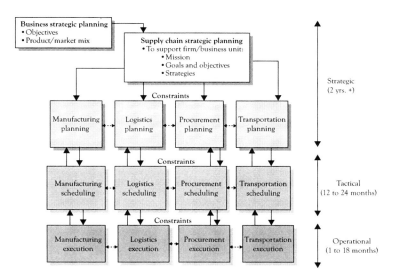

Figure 1.2. A unified business and supply chain planning framework.

The definition of what constitutes a major individual supply chain function will vary by firm. For example, some firms may consider transportation and/or customer service as components of their logistics organization, while other firms may not. Regardless of how many functions within a supply chain organization a firm chooses to define as major individual units, the framework in Figure 1.2 provides a well-defined, holistic organizational approach.

As described earlier in this chapter, this framework begins with the business strategic planning process. The goals and objectives developed at the business unit level establish requirements and define capabilities that the supply chain organization must provide to support business objectives. This facilitates the next strategic planning process where the supply chain organization formulates its overall mission, goals, objectives, and strategies. (Chapter 2 will describe a framework and methodology to facilitate this process.) The outputs of this process generate high level requirements and define capabilities that the individual functions within supply chain must then deliver. Further, the outputs of this process may also identify projects that can best help to achieve the plans developed at this overall supply chain level. At this point, individual functions such as manufacturing must initiate their own planning processes to map out the respective contributions that they will make in support of the overall supply chain plan.

At the individual function or department level, it is beneficial to delineate the future planning horizon into strategic, tactical, and operational planning buckets. Thus, each supply chain function has its own strategic, tactical, and operational planning processes. (Chapter 3 will explore this topic in detail.) To illustrate the different types of decisions and management controls exercised at each planning level, note in Figure 1.2 that at the tactical level we use "scheduling" as a function descriptor, while at the operational level "execution" is the function descriptor. In practice, at the tactical level one observes both planning and scheduling activities, while at the operational level, planning, scheduling, and execution activities all occur. Note also that while Figure 1.2 shows only four supply chain functions for illustrative purposes, some firms will have more than four major supply chain functions. Finally, in Figure 1.2 also note the following:

1. There are bi-directional vertical lines between the strategic, tactical, and operational planning levels of each supply chain function (e.g., manufacturing). A line emanating from a lower level to a higher level is known as a "feedback loop" in a hierarchical planning system. We will discuss feedback loops further in Chapter 3.
2. There are dashed horizontal lines between the individual functions. These lines illustrate that in practice, interactions in many forms should (and do) occur between individual supply chain functions. These interactions can be both formal (e.g., joint planning sessions) and informal (e.g., day-to-day communications).

In summary, the generic supply chain planning framework depicted in Figure 1.2 facilitates a firm-wide planning process whereby strategic plans initially formulated at the business unit level receive aligned planning, scheduling and execution support all the way down to the operational levels of each individual supply chain function.

Decision Support Systems and Performance Metrics

Now that we have introduced a unified, integrated process for business and supply chain planning, we need to discuss some key planning and control tools to facilitate this process. In this section, we briefly introduce two essential tools of a firm's planning and control processes:

1. *Decision Support Systems, and*
2. *Performance Measurement Systems.*

Each of these components will be discussed in depth later in the book (Chapters 4 and 5).

Decision support systems (DSS) for supply chain planning span a broad array of methodologies and techniques ranging from database analyses and data mining to simple spreadsheet-based analyses, to sophisticated mathematical optimization and simulation models, and statistical analyses. DSS represents a major field of study in itself. For our purposes, it is important to recognize that a firm must develop and maintain DSS tools to support activities at each level of its planning horizon (i.e., the strategic, tactical, and operational levels).

Performance measurement systems provide managers with indicators of how efficiently and effectively their supply chain is operating. Additionally, good performance measurement systems (PMS) also offer advance warnings or indications of potential future problems on a supply chain. A good PMS is also an absolute necessity to support the planning frameworks of a supply chain organization.

Figure 1.3 depicts the integral role that decision support and performance measurement systems play in the business and supply chain planning framework.

As illustrated, each individual supply chain function must have appropriate DSS tools at each level of its planning process. Similarly, each function must also have pertinent performance metrics to monitor its activities. And collectively, the supply chain organization must have the DSS and PMS tools required to manage the entire process. A firm with good supply chain frameworks, but which lacks the proper DSS and PMS tools cannot succeed. Similarly, a firm with strong DSS and PMS capabilities, but which lacks the appropriate supply chain frameworks to organize and utilize these tools cannot succeed. Only the combination of good

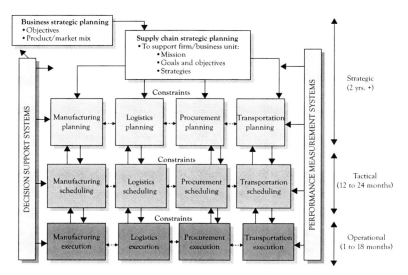

Figure 1.3. DSS and PMS integration into business and SC planning framework.

supply chain frameworks, complemented by strong decision support and performance measurement systems, will facilitate effective supply chain planning and successful operations.

Organization of the Book

The remainder of this book discusses all the components of the integrated framework, along with the application of DSS and PMS to support the planning processes as depicted in Figure 1.3. Chapter 2 begins with a framework for supply chain strategic planning. This chapter reviews a framework called the Mission, Objective, and Strategy (MOS) approach. As its name implies, a firm can employ this well-known strategic planning framework to develop the mission, objectives, and strategies of its supply chain function (or any other organization). In Chapter 2, we describe the MOS framework and then through a case study demonstrate how a supply chain organization can implement it in practice. Additionally, in the Appendix of this chapter we also review and demonstrate a powerful, yet easy-to-use multicriteria evaluation methodology called the Analytic Hierarchy Process[1] that helps a firm to prioritize potential strategic supply chain projects, and to assure that the selected projects align with the firm's objectives and strategies. Thus, Chapter 2 will arm an executive with a framework for supply chain strategic planning and its Appendix will demonstrate a methodology to select projects to carry out planned strategies.

Chapter 3 begins with further discussion of the rationale for employing hierarchical frameworks, and then presents a generic framework for hierarchical supply chain planning. A case study of an actual implementation by a firm of a hierarchical production and distribution planning framework follows. We will use this case study to examine how individual supply chain functions such as manufacturing and distribution can coordinate their planning activities at the strategic, tactical and operational levels. In this chapter, we review both tactical (annual) production planning methods and short run plant scheduling techniques, and we describe hierarchical approaches for linking long run and short run planning activities by means of feedback loops. In the second half of Chapter 3, we present examples of how individual supply chain functions such as transportation can construct their own hierarchical planning and scheduling frameworks. Additionally, we highlight the benefits for overall supply chain operations which result when each individual supply chain function maintains its own hierarchical planning framework. Chapter 3 concludes with an Appendix that further clarifies the concept of feedback loops via a tangible, detailed example.

Chapter 4 presents several case studies of Decision Support System implementations. The chapter begins with a general review of DSS including strategies for building comprehensive DSS to serve a supply chain group's strategic, tactical, and operational planning requirements. The case studies in Chapter 4 range from a global strategic and tactical manufacturing planning system to a daily operations inventory deployment system. Our discussion highlights the importance of integrating the supply chain DSS with a firm's ERP system, and the importance of maintaining a supply chain work force which can effectively utilize a DSS.

In Chapter 5, we examine frameworks for supply chain performance measurement. We begin with a general framework for supply chain performance metrics. Next we review the well-known Supply Chain Operations Reference (SCOR) model developed by the Supply Chain Council to monitor a firm's supply chain performance.[2] In the second half of the chapter, we introduce a methodology for linking the selection of a firm's key performance measures directly to its supply chain strategy. Finally, we conclude Chapter 5 by demonstrating a straightforward, yet innovative methodology by which executives can create a customized management index to monitor their supply chain's performance.

Chapter 6 concludes the book with a brief summary, followed by final thoughts and recommendations on how practitioners can incorporate the frameworks and tools presented in this book into their own supply chain planning and management processes.

Appendix 1A: Additional Background on Hierarchical Planning Frameworks

This Appendix offers additional discussion of the rationale for a hierarchical planning framework, and of the distinction between the types of decisions required at the strategic, tactical, and operational planning levels.

The motivation and rationale for employing a hierarchical planning and scheduling process for a supply chain function can best be understood by first briefly considering a general framework for managerial decision-making. In his seminal work on planning and control systems, Robert Anthony (1965)[3] presented a planning framework often cited and utilized by both theoreticians and practitioners.

Anthony classified all managerial decisions into three broad categories consisting of: (1) strategic planning, (2) management control, and (3) operational control. A number of authors (e.g., Ackoff, 1970)[4] have termed the second category as tactical planning and the third category as operational planning and scheduling. For purposes of this book, we will denote these three categories as strategic planning, tactical planning and operational planning. Additionally, we note that tactical planning encompasses both planning and scheduling, while operational planning includes planning, scheduling and execution activities. The planning framework that we present is hierarchical because the results of each planning process guide and direct the planning process at the next lower level. That is, the results of strategic planning guide and direct tactical planning, while tactical planning results guide and direct operational planning.[5]

Strategic Planning

Strategic planning represents the highest level of the hierarchy of decision-making activities which occur within a firm or a major function (e.g., a supply chain function such as manufacturing). Ultimately, strategic planning decisions, whether they take place at the business, supply chain, or supply chain function levels, are all concerned with defining the long-term objectives of a firm or a function, charting the long term course that will allow the achievement of defined objectives, and assuring that the proper resources and assets necessary to support long term objectives are allocated. In his framework, Anthony (1965) offers the following definition of the role of strategic planning. He states that strategic planning is "the process of deciding on objectives of the

- Plant and warehouse locations and missions (i.e., network infrastructure and design)
- New plant locations and sizes, and plant closings
- New warehouse locations and sizes, and warehouse closings
- Plant and warehouse capacity and technology design
- Mix of owned assets vs. third party resources utilized (i.e., outsourcing decisions)
- Transportation network design
- Order fulfillment approach (e.g., make-to-order vs. make-to-stock)
- Global vs. regional vs. local procurement sourcing

Figure 1A.1. Selected strategic supply chain function decisions.

organization, on changes in these objectives, on the resources used to obtain these objectives, and on the policies that are to govern the acquisition, use and disposition of these resources." In supply chain planning functions, there are a number of classic decisions which generally fall into the strategic planning category. For illustrative purposes, Figure 1A.1 displays a sample of typical strategic logistics and supply chain function issues and problems which firms must address.

Tactical Planning

Tactical planning represents the second or intermediate level of decision making activities that occur in a firm or a function. Quite often annual planning is viewed as a subset of tactical planning. In Anthony's (1965) framework, the decision-making process primarily focuses on resource allocation and resource utilization at this level. Anthony describes that managers' tactical planning activities must obtain and use resources effectively and efficiently to assure the accomplishment of the firm or function's objectives. This description seems quite intuitive when considered in the context of a planning hierarchy. For example, strategic planning decisions address such supply chain issues as infrastructure and overall capacity levels. Thus, at the next level down, the decision-making process must focus on how to most effectively utilize the infrastructure and capacity that the implementation of strategic decisions has created. Figure 1A.2 offers a sampling of some of the more common tactical supply chain function decisions.

- Assignment of production capacity to product families, by plant, by medium size time periods (e.g., quarters)
- Planned manufacturing capacity utilization rates, by plant and network wide
- Workforce requirements (regular and overtime levels)
- Plant—distribution center—sales region/country sourcing assignments
- Inter-facility (e.g., inter-distribution center) shipment plans
- Transportation carrier selections
- Selection of materials suppliers by region and product

Figure 1A.2. Selected tactical supply chain function decisions.

Operational Planning

Operational planning and scheduling represents the third and lowest level of the hierarchical planning process. At this level, the firm must carry out the resource allocation and utilization decisions previously made at the tactical level in the daily and weekly activities which occur at the operational level. Responsibilities of managers at this level consist of assuring that the organization performs individual tasks efficiently and effectively, and that these tasks support the higher level tactical plans of the organization. Again this framework seems intuitively appealing from a hierarchical perspective. At the tactical level, the firm makes the resource allocation decisions to facilitate the operations of the business, and at the operational level, the firm executes its daily operations using the resources made available by the tactical planning process. For illustrative purposes, Figure 1A.3 presents a sample of these types of decisions.

- Daily and weekly production scheduling at the item level
- Customer order processing and scheduling
- Warehouse operations scheduling
- Labor scheduling for manufacturing and warehouse operations
- Vehicle scheduling
- Materials acquisition scheduling

Figure 1A.3. Selected operational supply chain function decisions.

CHAPTER 2

Supply Chain Strategic Planning

Introduction

In this chapter we discuss the supply chain strategic planning process, whose purpose is to provide clear direction for the organization's supply chain activities over the next two to five years. As mentioned in Chapter 1, the supply chain strategic planning process must be in consonance with the overall business strategic planning process, and so it must be supportive of market share and profitability goals, along with business and product mix targets. In this way, the supply chain strategic plan is directed toward improving business performance.

We offer a proven framework that can support the strategic planning process and that can also be applied to help the organization allocate its scarce resources to specific projects that will support the achievement of its strategy. This framework was successfully applied at Warner Lambert and Pfizer when one of the authors served as a director of logistics for these organizations and the other consulted on their implementation. As we describe and illustrate through a fictitious company, this framework offers a well-defined process by which firms can identify those projects that will contribute most significantly toward achieving their objectives and executing their strategies. Before presenting the details of the planning framework, we begin by discussing some of the fundamental components of supply chain strategy that a firm may consider in formulating its strategic supply chain plans.

Supply Chain and Logistics Strategy Concepts

The supply chain planning process begins with the formulation of an overall strategy that should be based on the characteristics of the product

·ved. Products can be categorized as either functional or
~nding on the predictability of demand, size of margins,
.. µroduct life cycles, and level of product variety. Functional
products face a stable demand process and low margins, and so their
supply chains should focus on cost efficiency. Innovative products face
unpredictable demand but have higher margins, and so a responsive strategy is desired, and can be achieved using mass customization or product
postponement (also called delayed differentiation).[1]

Characteristics of the supply processes, including the number of
supply sources and process changes, and variable or stable yields can
also be related to the choice of a supply chain strategy. Products having
predictable demand and stable supply sources may require an efficient
supply chain strategy, while those having unpredictable demand and
stable supply sources may require a responsive strategy. However, when
demand is predictable and the supply process is evolving, a risk hedging
strategy might be employed to pool resources to share risks in supply
disruption. An agile supply chain is needed when demand is unpredictable
and supply is evolving. It must be flexible enough to respond to changing
levels of demand, while trying to minimize the supply disruptions.[2]

Important components of an overall supply chain strategy are the
logistics strategies related to planning, material acquisition, production,
and product delivery. Previous research identified three logistic strategic
orientations: process, market, and information strategies. Process strategy
focuses on managing logistic activities with a goal of controlling costs and is
related to the cost efficiency strategy. Market strategy focuses on managing
logistic activities across business units in order to reduce complexity faced
by customers and is somewhat related to the responsive strategy. The
third, information strategy, has the goal of achieving inter-organizational
coordination and collaboration throughout the channel.[3] Interestingly,
further research showed that the importance of these three strategies and
their outcomes (logistics coordination effectiveness, customer service
commitment, and company/division competitiveness) was found not to
vary by an amount greater than chance during an 18-year time period.
Those firms classified as pursuing an intense logistics strategy (i.e., place
greater importance on process, market, and information strategies)
increased from 52.5% in 1990 to 61.0% in 1999 to 71.4% in 2008.

In addition, process strategy was found to be relatively more important than market strategy, with both more important than information strategy.[4]

Other researchers developed a classification scheme for logistics strategy types based on the results of a survey of managers and executives knowledgeable about their firm's logistics strategies. Two strategies emerged: functional logistics and externally oriented logistics. Those firms taking a functional logistics strategy focus on inventory and order management, order processing, procurement, and storage. The underlying measurement items emphasize efficiency and cost management, analysis, and control. This strategy is similar to the process strategy previously discussed. Those firms employing an externally oriented strategy are most concerned with ensuring that their logistics activities are compatible with the needs of their trading partners and/or directed toward stewardship of the overall business environment (e.g., green or socially responsible logistics). Firms adopting this strategy focus more on coordination and collaboration, social responsibility, strategic distribution planning and technology and information systems. This strategy is somewhat related to the information strategy previously discussed. Customer service, operational controls, and transportation management did not vary significantly between the functional and externally oriented strategies.[5]

In situations where a product is in the stable or decline phase of its life cycle, opportunities may exist to extend the product by selling it in a new geographic market where it begins anew in the growth phase. Here the supply chain will likely initially require a responsive strategy since demand will be somewhat uncertain at entry, or perhaps an agile strategy, if there is significant supply risk. The firm will also likely initially follow a market logistics strategy. Once market experience is gained and as demand is better understood, then the supply chain strategy for a functional product can transition from responsive to cost efficiency, or risk hedging if significant supply risk still remains. An externally oriented logistics strategy may be selected if stewardship issues have great prominence in the local market.

To summarize, whether products are functional or innovative, and whether the supply process is stable or evolving, are important considerations in supply chain strategy development. Cost efficiency, responsiveness to customers, and the need to hedge on key resources result from such considerations. The supply chain strategy should address internal functions, such as manufacturing, inventory control, and procurement, as well as external functions and relationships, including coordination with the firm's channel partners, as well as the supply chain's impact on society and the environment. How these factors are brought together into a coherent supply chain strategy will now be considered. As we shall see, they affect the choice and relative importance of specific supply chain objectives and strategies directed toward achieving the overall mission.

Setting the Stage for Planning

To illustrate our planning framework we use as an example a fictitious firm, Zenith Industries. This example is based on our previous experience with firms that have successfully employed this approach. Zenith produces a wide variety of consumer goods and distributes its products to a broad array of retailers, who then sell these goods to consumers. Recently, the company has also implemented its own direct-to-consumer channel of distribution, an effort still in initial stages of development. Zenith's supply chain organization is just now entering its annual strategic planning process.

The first step is to form a supply chain planning team, consisting of a mix of senior and mid-level supply chain managers. The team may include executives from the supply chain and logistics organizations, marketing, customer service, manufacturing, procurement, and transportation, among others, with the exact mix depending on the specifics of the organizational structure. The planning process can be organized into three phases:

1. Review the business strategic plan and perform an environmental scan
2. Develop the supply chain mission, objectives, and strategy
3. Identify and select specific projects or activities that enable the execution of the strategy

We will discuss each of these phases in turn.

Phase 1: Business Strategy Review and Environmental Scan

The supply chain planning team begins the first phase by reviewing the business strategic plan, which may already be completed or near completion. The idea is to begin thinking about how the supply chain can support overall business strategies and objectives. For example, an objective to increase the firm's profitability as measured by EBITDA (earnings before interest, taxes, depreciation, and amortization) may imply, for example, the need to reduce supply chain cost and/or to increase revenue by offering better customer delivery service to capture more market share. The key point is that the planning team must develop a supply chain strategy that supports the business strategy.

Next, the planning team needs to perform an "environmental scan" to obtain relevant information on the business environment in which their supply chain operates. The purpose of the "environmental scan" is to identify those economic, political, social, and technological events and trends that will influence the successful operation of the supply chain. The range of trends, factors, and initiatives that a firm must consider in crafting its supply chain strategy increases every year at an accelerating pace. The rapid advance of supply chain technologies, globalization of supply chains and competition, environmental and sustainability initiatives, supply chain security and regulatory issues, global IT systems, and product nomenclature represent just a sampling of the many considerations that render supply chain planning an extremely complex undertaking. The economic environment includes the trends in the macro economy at large and its impact on suppliers, customers, and the eventual consumers, as well as the micro economy in which the firm competes. Some examples include changes in the availability of key materials, exchange rates, level of competition, number of competitors, and customer mix, as well as expectations for supply chain performance. Plans and strategies should not be created in a vacuum—it is important to have a solid grasp on the internal and external environment of the supply chain. Armed with the information gained, we can move on to Phase 2.[6]

Phase 2: Mission, Objectives, Strategy[7]

A simple but effective planning approach is to develop the supply chain's mission, objectives, and strategy (MOS).[8] As shown in Figure 2.1, the MOS approach requires that the planning team defines the supply chain's overall mission (*step 1*), establishes objectives to support its mission (*step 2*), and then develops strategies to support its objectives (*step 3*). The purpose of stating the mission is to define the supply chain's overall goal, provide a sense of direction, and help guide its actions. The mission provides the context in which the supply chain's objectives are formulated. In developing its objectives, the planning team focuses on the set of functional capabilities that their supply chain must have in order to facilitate carrying out its mission.

In the third planning stage, the team develops strategies designed to meet those objectives posed in the second stage. To design their strategies the planning team must consider and address the needs of all of the major stakeholders and constituents of the firm and its supply chain. Thus, the firm formulates strategies that will drive its approach toward its consumers, its customers, the governmental and societal entities the firm interacts with, its financial responsibilities, its supply chain suppliers and partners, and its internal employees and operations.

The supply chain planning team considered several possible statements of its supply chain mission, including:

Create and sustain a competitive advantage for Zenith by enabling its supply chain to provide exceptional customer value

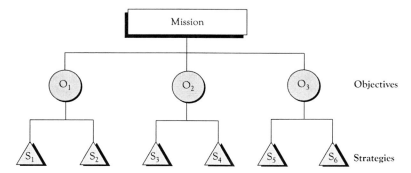

Figure 2.1. The mission, objective and strategy (MOS) approach to strategic planning.

Position Zenith's supply chain to provide high quality products with extraordinary service to its customers

After much deliberation, the planning team defined the supply chain mission as:

Supply Chain Mission: *Position Zenith's supply chain to support the overall firm objectives as efficiently and effectively as possible*

As this mission statement underscores, Zenith's supply chain management views its role as one of facilitating and enhancing the firm's ability to compete successfully in its industry. Then based upon this mission, and the knowledge gained from phase 1, the planning team defined explicit *performance objectives* in the following areas:

- Regulatory Compliance
- Cost Efficiency
- Delivery Effectiveness
- Flexibility
- Security

Relating to our previous discussion in the Supply Chain and Logistics Strategy Concepts section, supply chain efficiency and responsiveness were highlighted, and are reflected in three of the objectives (cost efficiency, delivery effectiveness, and flexibility). In addition, reflective of the external supply chain strategic orientation discussed, regulatory compliance and security were included as objectives.

In practice the planning team should formulate precise objectives against which it can accurately evaluate itself in the defined areas. Objectives should be measureable, achievable, flexible, and consistent with the plan being developed. Thus, for each objective a metric must be specified so that progress toward achieving the objective can be tracked. Some examples are given in Table 2.1.

One more observation about supply chain objectives: in the process of setting objectives, firms often need to consider the related tradeoffs. In the case of Zenith, tradeoffs certainly need to be discussed with regard to the objectives of cost efficiency, delivery effectiveness, and flexibility (responsiveness) to customer needs. The remaining two objectives—regulatory compliance and security—relate more to the external environment in which the supply

Table 2.1. Supply Chain Objectives Defined with Metrics

Objective	Definition with metric
Regulatory Compliance	No violations of laws relating to product transportation and shipment
Cost Efficiency	Reduce logistics costs per case by 5%
Delivery Effectiveness	Deliver 99% of all items by the targeted date
Flexibility	Respond to 99% of changes in customer orders within one day of receipt
Security	No physical or cyber security breaches

chain operates. With these two objectives, as with the others, Zenith must weigh all appropriate actions and tradeoffs.

After developing its five major objectives, Zenith then considered the specific strategies needed to achieve its objectives in a way that met the needs of its major stakeholders and supply chain constituents. Specifically, the supply chain planning team determined that it needed to develop **supply chain strategies** that focused on six key areas:

- The Consumer (CONS)
- The Customers (CUST)
- Governmental and Societal Responsibilities (G&S)
- Financial Well-Being (FIN)
- Suppliers and Partners (S&P)
- Internal Operations and Employees (OPS&E)

This set of strategies incorporates all of Zenith's stakeholders and constituents, both internal and external to the firm. In practice, explicit statements must be developed for each of these strategies. For example, a typical customer strategy might be *to enhance the customers' perception of Zenith*. This could be a key component of the company's overall "customer" strategy. As another example, the government and societal strategy might be to become a green supply chain, specifically by focusing on reducing energy consumption and increasing recycling efforts. Explicit statements would be developed for all the remaining strategies to complete Phase 2.

The mission, objectives, and strategies defined by Zenith's supply chain management provide a framework for the organization to move forward. The MOS framework as applied to Zenith is presented as levels 1–3 in

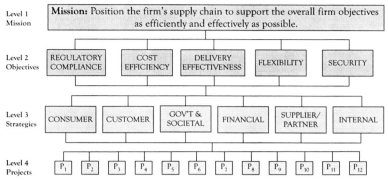

Figure 2.2. Supply chain strategic planning framework.

Figure 2.2. We now turn to Phase 3 (level 4 in Figure 2.2), selecting specific projects or activities that enable the execution of the strategies developed.

Phase 3: Identifying and Selecting Projects

Zenith now must select and initiate individual action plans or projects that will facilitate the successful implementation of its strategies. Without execution, the strategizing is hollow and of minimal value. This effort consists of first identifying a set of potential supply chain strategic projects, and then from that broader set, selecting the actual projects to be pursued that best help to achieve the strategy.

As shown in Figure 1.2 from Chapter 1, strategic projects could represent significant changes in functional areas of the supply chain network, such as adding new facilities or expanding/reducing capacity; modifying the transportation mode or network design; moving from local to global procurement; outsourcing a supply chain activity or process; and changing the order fulfillment approach from make-to-stock to make-to-order; among others. When the firm performs individual supply chain function planning (e.g., manufacturing planning), such projects typically will be addressed in detail at that level. We assume that this is the case, and will address these issues in Chapter 3. Here we focus on projects that may address trends and topics that are known to be of current importance to supply chain managers across multiple functional areas and that support contemporary strategies across these functions. In other words, this phase of the supply chain strategic planning process considers projects that will significantly impact multiple functions of the supply chain.

A comprehensive set of supply chain trends and potential project areas that a firm might consider during its strategic planning process is given as Figure 2.3. This list is based on: (1) a review of all articles published in nine representative supply chain trade magazines and journals in a recent

---

1 Business Intelligence and Analytics—level of emphasis, future directions
2 Carbon Footprint—Does firm measure this today? if so, how? Future strategy?
3 Clarity of the Supply Chain (SC) Management Responsibilities within Firm
4 Cold Chain—Future trends and requirements (particularly for pharma and biologic product distribution)
5 Collaborative Planning, Forecasting and Replenishment (CPFR)
6 Control of Inbound Transportation—Larger firms (manufacturers) increasing their efforts to control inbound (i.e., suppliers') transportation, as well as outbound transportation—future trends?
7 Cross-Docking and Minimizing Logistics "touch" strategies—future direction?
8 Current Economic Downturn—impact, if any, on long term SC strategies?
9 Customer Relationship Management (CRM) strategy and its evolution
10 Customer Segmentation Strategies including customer profitability & Activity Based Costing (ABC) analyses
11 Demand Visibility—Use of POS (point of sale) Data
12 Direct Store Delivery—Manufacturers' strategies to minimize the "number of touches" in logistics operations
13 Direct to Consumer Delivery and Internet Order Management
14 Forecast Accuracy and Demand Management Initiatives
15 Fuel Price Volatility—impact on SC design and strategy
16 General Logistics Strategy or "Philosophy" of firm -->. a. Focused on maximizing efficiency—i.e., "functionally oriented", or b. Focused on maintaining flexibility to react rapidly to changing customer demands—i.e., "externally oriented", or c. Weighted mix of the two strategies
17 Global DC and Plant (i.e., Facilities) Design Strategies—for large-scale firms is best strategy to take a standardized approach in warehouse and/or plant design, or should each DC and plant design be based on local/regional needs?
18 Global Standards strategies of firm—including support for EDI, UPC, GTIN and related nomenclatures and data sets
19 Global Trade Management (GTM)—evolution of GTM? Will GTM become better integrated into firms' SC Organizations in the future?
20 Green and Sustainability Initiatives. Evolution? Next steps for individual firms?
21 Hazardous materials handling and storage strategies
22 Impact of the Globalization of SCs on Risk and SC Vulnerability. How should firms address these issues?
23 Import/Export Compliance requirements and organizational capabilities
24 Import Duties—impact on SC Design
25 Increased Use of Intermodal Transportation
26 Information Technology (IT) Strategies
27 Inventory Investment and deployment strategies
28 Information Technology Investment in SC/Logistics Operations
29 Labor Productivity Strategies (for plant and warehouse operations)
30 Lean Logistics—What is firm's strategy?

Figure 2.3. Supply chain topic areas and trends.—(Continued)

31 Marketing/Logistics Interface—tactics, strategies to assure an effective relationship
32 Nonfossil fuel and recycled waste energy strategies
33 Off-Shoring vs. Near Shoring (or Right Shoring)
34 Operations Research Tools To Support SC Operations—what is optimal level of resource allocation to these capabilities by firm?
35 Other Internal Dept Collaborations in SC Operations—what will be trends, new initiatives
36 Outsourcing Strategies
37 Performance Measurement & Dashboard Strategies
38 Ports in the U.S.—West coast highly congested, however east coast ports have capacity/depth issues, Panama Canal capacity expansion: implications for firm's transport and related strategies
39 Postponement SC Strategies: (1) time postponement (2) place postponement
40 Procurement/Sourcing—How far back should a firm review its supply chain sources? Direct suppliers, suppliers' suppliers?
41 Product Packaging Strategies including re-usable packaging approaches
42 Rationale For Global Supply Chains—what drives a firm to establish global SCs and will this trend continue to move forward unabated?
43 Recycling Strategies
44 Reverse Logistics/Product Returns. Current and future strategies?
45 RFID Strategies and use of RFID vs. use of multidimension Bar Codes
46 Risk Management role in SC Strategy & Operations—will this continue to become more critical?
47 S&OP—Sales & Operations Planning—Future Trends and Directions
48 SC "Skill Set Requirements" to manage Global SCs. What does firm need?
49 SC Design Approach—Explore two different concepts for how SCs develop: a. As a "natural phenomenon" where a firm links up with other firms that already have major links—and a SC evolves; or b. As a "managed SC" where a large firm in the most literal sense orchestrates the entire supply by selecting the other participants in the SC—rather than letting its (the large firm's) suppliers select their partners
50 SC Human Capital Investment—trends in training, education, etc.
51 SC Innovation Strategies—how to promote innovation within firm's SC organization
52 SC Network and Operations Flexibility and Responsiveness Initiatives
53 SC Pressure Points—what are they for firm, and what will they be in future?
54 SC Strategic Planning Methodology Initiatives—e.g., use of Scenario Planning
55 Six Sigma And Other Improvement Programs—current and future emphasis on these programs
56 Supplier Relationship Management (SRM) strategies
57 Supply Chain (SC) Security strategies
58 Supply Chain Social Capital Initiatives/Emphasis—the concept here is that a large firm or a SC of multiple firms actively facilitates "socialization" among other participants on the collective SC—i.e., promotes collaboration, "getting to know each other" among other firms on the total SC. Is this an initiative/trend we can expect to observe more of in the future? Should a firm pursue this approach?
59 Tax Strategies—Impact of taxes and transfer pricing on SC network design
60 Third Party Logistics (3PL)—increasing use of 3PLs; will this continue? Future trends? Is 3PL the right strategy for a firm?
61 Total Delivered (Landed) Costs Approach. Is a firm with an international SC using true landed costs in its decision-making process?
62 Warehouse and Plant Automation Investment—future direction? What level is right for a firm?

Figure 2.3. Supply chain topic areas and trends.

12-month period;[9] (2) a review of a list of logistics tactics and strategies, based on interviews with industry practitioners, that appears in a recent publication;[10] and (3) a series of informal discussions with supply chain practitioners. In practice, potential projects could emanate from such a formalized review process, the planning team's assessment of the firm's supply chain needs, or even better, a combination of the two approaches. But regardless of the approach taken, establishing a topic list helps to ensure that the firm's strategic planning process is comprehensive and does not become too narrow or inwardly focused. During the planning process the number of potential project areas and specific projects will be reduced to a manageable subset that can be evaluated more closely. Since resources are limited, the firm must prioritize the remaining projects based on benefit-cost considerations.

Returning to Zenith's strategic planning process, Figure 2.4 displays the list of potential supply chain projects that the planning team has proposed to support their strategies, objectives, and ultimately their mission. For ease of illustration, we have indicated that each potential project supports just one strategy. For example, project 11, expand import/export compliance IT capabilities, supports the Government and Society (G&S) strategy. In practice, however, one project often supports multiple strategies, which our framework can easily accommodate. In this case, Zenith's managers developed the potential project list after considering whether they sufficiently support the execution of the specific strategies developed. Additionally, in constructing its initial list, Zenith's managers made certain that they identified at least one potential project that supports each of the six strategies. Note that these 12 projects are the fourth, or lowest level, of the supply chain strategic planning framework introduced earlier (Figure 2.2).

Using Figure 2.2 as a guide, Zenith's supply chain strategic planning team engages in discussion and debate to determine the importance of the stated objectives (level 2) in achieving the supply chain mission (level 1). If they wish, they can formalize this process by applying a simple technique of allocating100 points across the five objectives. Next, the team considers the extent to which the defined strategies (level 3) meet each of the objectives (level 2), by allocating each objective's points across the strategies.

For example, the planning team might allocate 25 points to the cost efficiency objective based on its importance in achieving the supply chain

	Project description	Strategy project supports
1	Streamline existing direct-to-consumer delivery and Internet ordering services.	CONS
2	Integrate POS data as input to current forecasting and production scheduling processes.	CUST
3	Establish and enhance customer relationship management (CRM) services.	CUST
4	Implement customer segmentation program based on customer profitability and activity-based costing (ABC) analyses.	CUST
5	Expand supplier relationship management (SRM) programs.	S&P
6	Evaluate and benchmark supply chain security processes and procedures and recommend enhancements.	G&S
7	Integrate individual country sales and operations planning processes into one Global S&OP process.	OPS&E
8	Develop and implement plan to optimize use of RFID in the supply chain.	OPS&E
9	Evaluate current use of 3PLs and recommend if usage should be increased.	FIN
10	Develop and implement labor productivity measurement systems for plant and warehouse operations.	OPS&E
11	Expand import/export compliance IT capabilities.	G&S
12	Benchmark current carbon footprint and develop long-term green manufacturing operations plan.	G&S

Figure 2.4. Zenith's potential supply chain projects and strategies supported.

mission. Assuming the financial and internal strategies support this objective, they might be allocated 15 and 10 points, respectively, based on their relative degree of support. Totaling the points for each strategy determines its overall importance in achieving the mission. Following the framework, the planning team now has linked its objectives to its mission, its strategies to its objectives, and its strategies to its mission (via the strategies link to the objectives).

The strategic planning process generates significant additional value when plans lead to specific actions. Thus, a candidate set of projects is evaluated next (see Figure 2.4). Zenith understands the importance of allocating their limited resources to those projects that best support the most important strategies. The projects are ranked based on the extent to which they support the achievement of strategies. For example, assuming that the customer strategy (CUST) has a score of 20, and the planning team believes that project 3 (CRM services—from Figure 2.4) very strongly supports this strategy, they might elect to score project 3 at the 90% level, and so allocate it a score of 18 (0.90*20). On the other hand, project 2, integrate POS data, although important is deemed to be somewhat less critical in supporting CUST, and is scored at the 75% level for a value of 15 (0.75*20). This idea can easily be extended to the situation where individual projects support multiple strategies—simply add the points obtained from each strategy the project supports. The projects are ranked according to their total score, and then can be funded in order starting with the highest until the budget is exhausted.

At the conclusion of Phase 3, the planning team communicates the results of the MOS process and project funding decisions to everyone in the supply chain function as well as to relevant personnel in other parts of the organization. The objective here is to let everyone know where the emphasis needs to be placed in running the business. The strategic discussion should, in fact, lead to the subsequent development of tactical and operational plans that best achieve the mission. We discuss this further in Chapter 3.

In conducting planning meetings, it is useful to have members of the supply chain planning team prioritize or weight the various items individually without first discussing them among the group. This approach assures that all individuals actively participate in the process and increases the probability that all participants will "buy-into" the planning framework. It also encourages individual creativity and initiative while ensuring that the views of all team members are considered. In short, this approach enhances the prospects for success. The ultimate goal is to achieve agreement and alignment at the various steps of the planning process so that the team concludes the process united in their support of the prioritized strategies and projects.

Of course it is not absolutely necessary to use a scoring approach like the one outlined above, but it is helpful to minimize the subjectivity and the influence of the most dominant individuals in making the project selection decisions. However, in some instances, a firm may wish to use a more formal process to prioritize the strategies, objectives, and projects. The Analytic Hierarchy Process (AHP), developed by Thomas Saaty and described in his book, *The Analytic Hierarchy Process,*[11] is an easy-to-use decision making method for prioritizing alternatives such as projects when multiple levels of factors must be considered.[12] The Appendix to this chapter provides more details on how this approach can be implemented through easy-to-use decision support software.

Conclusion: Making Better Decisions

The framework we have presented is designed to support a firm's supply chain strategic planning activities and its project selection process. Our framework utilizes the mission, objectives, and strategies (MOS) approach for strategic supply chain planning and links the results to the project identification and selection process. In the business supply chain planning process, where managers are required to make difficult and often budget-constrained decisions concerning which projects to implement, the framework presented here offers the guidance necessary to assure aligned decision-making. Specifically, the explicit links between projects and strategies, strategies and objectives, and objectives and the supply chain mission facilitate clear and consistent decision-making.

Finally, as illustrated in Figure 2.2, the framework promotes a comprehensive and structured approach to the supply chain strategic planning process.

Appendix 2A: Decision Support for Supply Chain Strategic Planning

The Analytic Hierarchy Process (AHP) can be applied to help the supply chain planning team determine the importance of the objectives and strategies in achieving the mission, the alignment of the action plans or projects in achieving the strategies, and ultimately, the supply chain mission. Using the results of the AHP analysis, a benefit-cost analysis can then be performed to determine the project portfolio that is best aligned with the strategic planning process. We illustrate the application of the

AHP approach to the strategic planning process using the Zenith example described in Chapter 2.

Applying the AHP Approach to Mission, Objectives, and Strategy

The AHP is a decision making method for prioritizing alternatives when multiple factors must be considered.[13] This approach allows the decision maker to structure problems in the form of a hierarchy or a set of integrated levels, such as, the goal, the criteria, and the alternatives. We first apply the AHP to Phase 2 of the supply chain strategic planning process as discussed in Chapter 2, where the goal is achieving the supply chain mission, the criteria are the objectives, and the alternatives are the supply chain strategies. Specifically, the AHP analysis will determine the relative importance of the objectives in achieving the mission, the strategies in achieving the objectives, and then combining both results, the strategies in achieving the mission of the supply chain organization. Later we will connect this AHP analysis with Phase 3, identifying and selecting projects.

A series of expert judgments from the planning team are needed to drive the AHP analysis. All of the individuals participating in the supply chain strategic planning process could reach a consensus and that judgment would be used. Alternatively, each individual could enter their own set of judgments, and these would be combined across all participants. We assume that one set of consensus judgments are provided. All judgments are solicited in the form of *pairwise comparisons,* meaning that we will always be comparing two items at a time. An AHP analysis uses pairwise comparisons to measure the impact of items on one level of the hierarchy on the next higher level. As Figure 2.2 illustrates, in the supply chain strategic planning process, mission is the level above objectives and so we first wish to determine the impact of objectives on the mission. For example, the AHP analysis asks the question: "With respect to achieving the mission, which objective is more important, regulatory compliance or cost efficiency, and how much more important is it?" The AHP measurement scale given as Figure 2A.1 is used to specify the value of pairwise comparisons. For example, if cost efficiency is between equally and moderately more important than regulatory compliance in achieving the

Intensity of importance	Definition	Explanation
1	Equal	Two activities contribute equally to the objective.
3	Moderate importance	Experience and judgment slightly favor one activity over another.
5	Strong importance	Experience and judgment strongly favor one activity over another.
7	Very strong or demonstrated importance	An activity is favored very strongly over another or its dominance has been demonstrated in practice.
9	Extreme importance	The evidence favoring one activity over another is of the highest possible order of affirmation.
2, 4, 6, 8	For compromise between the above values	Sometimes one needs to interpolate a compromise judgment numerically because there is no good word to describe it.
1.1–1.9	For tied activities	When elements are close and nearly indistinguishable; moderate is 1.3 and extreme is 1.9.
Reciprocals of above	If activity A has one of the above numbers assigned to it when compared with activity B, then B has the reciprocal value when compared to A.	For example, if the pairwise comparison of A to B is 3.0, then the pairwise comparison of B to A is 1/3.

Figure 2A.1. AHP 1–9 measurement scale.

mission, a "2" would represent this judgment. If one changes the order of comparison and compares regulatory compliance with cost efficiency, then the reciprocal of 2, or ½, would be the appropriate judgment. Either numbers or words can be used to enter judgments in AHP software such as *Decision Lens Suite*.[14] Figure 2A.2 is a Decision Lens screenshot illustrating the process of entering a cost efficiency-regulatory compliance pairwise comparison.

We have five objectives, and so to cover all possible pairs of objectives we would like to obtain 10 (i.e., 5(4)/2) pairwise comparisons. However, the number of required judgments can be reduced to 4 (i.e., 5–1) if necessary (i.e., cost efficiency to regulatory compliance, regulatory

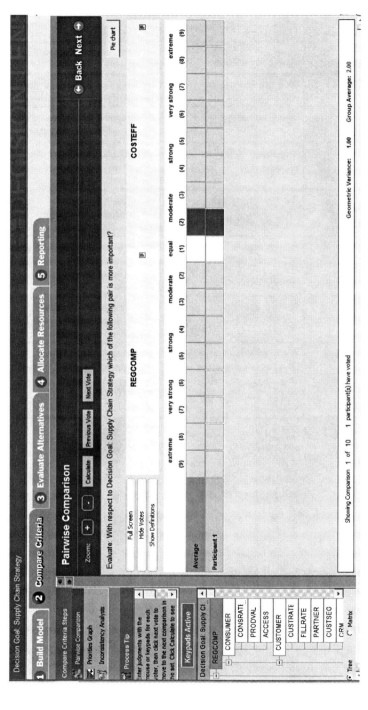

Figure 2A.2. Decision lens screenshot: Entering a pairwise comparison between regulatory compliance and cost efficiency.

compliance to delivery effectiveness, delivery effectiveness to flexibility, flexibility to security). The additional judgments simply help to improve accuracy. At each level such as objectives, the weights of the items being compared are determined by a mathematical algorithm and will sum to 1. For example, it might turn out that the weight of cost efficiency in achieving the mission is 0.250, while the weight of regulatory compliance is 0.078. The resulting objective weights are shown on level 2 of Figure 2A.3.

The next step of the AHP process is to determine the extent to which the strategies achieve the objectives. The six strategies must be pairwise compared with respect to *each* of the five objectives. If a strategy does not support a particular objective, then the strategy is not evaluated with respect to that particular objective. The AHP approach might ask, "With respect to achieving the cost efficiency objective, which strategy is more important, financial or government and society, and how much more important is it?" After pairwise comparing all of the strategies with respect to the cost efficiency objective, we might determine, for example, that the financial strategy has a 0.380 weight (out of a possible 1.000) in achieving this objective. Assuming that the cost efficiency objective has a weight of 0.250 in achieving the mission, then the financial strategy is entitled to a portion, $0.380*0.250 = 0.095$, of the 0.250 cost efficiency weight. However, since the financial strategy might support the other four objectives to varying degrees, its final weight in supporting the mission will be determined only by summing up its *contributions to all five objectives* (0.161 on level 3 in Figure 2A.3). In this way we can obtain weights for the objectives in achieving the mission, and then for strategies in achieving the mission.

The complete AHP hierarchy for our supply chain strategic planning example is given in Figure 2A.3. The results show that delivery effectiveness is the most importance objective, with a weight of 0.354, followed by cost efficiency with a weight of 0.250. In terms of strategies, the government and society strategy with a weight of 0.380 is the most important, followed by the internal strategy with a weight of 0.206. This completes the application of the AHP to Phase 2 of the supply chain strategic planning process.

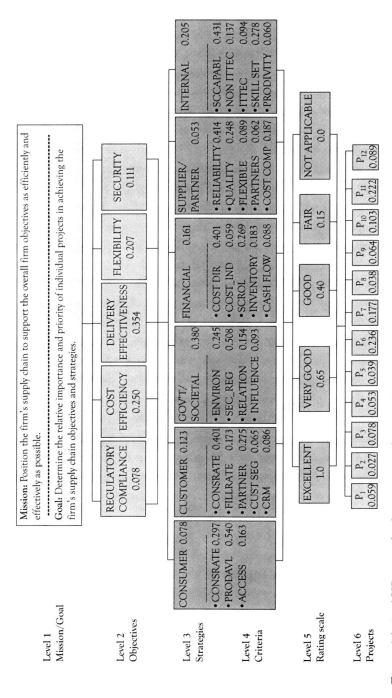

Figure 2A.3. AHP—supply chain strategy framework.

Apply the AHP to Strategic Project Selection

As described in Chapter 2, Phase 3 of the strategic planning process begins with identifying potential strategic projects, which in Zenith's situation are the 12 projects identified in Chapter 2 (Figure 2.4). Now we determine how to select those projects that best achieve the supply chain mission. Rather than evaluate the projects directly in terms of their ability to achieve the strategies, we first develop a set of evaluative criteria for each strategy. These criteria can be thought of as specific measures that directly relate to a given strategy. The better a project achieves a strategy's criteria, the higher its weight or score.

The criteria for each strategy are shown as level 4 in Figure 2A.3 and are defined in Figure 2A.4. For example, an AHP question might be: "With respect to achieving the government/societal strategy, how much more important is compliance level with all federal, state and local government environmental laws (ENVIRON) as compared to compliance level with all applicable governmental security and regulatory laws and agencies such as Homeland Security, OSHA and FDA (SEC_REG)?" Note that the criteria used to evaluate each strategy are pairwise compared to only these other criteria which support the same strategy. Thus, the three criteria (CONSRATE, PRODAVL, and ACCESS) at level 4 under the consumer strategy (level 3) have weights that sum to 1. These weights reflect the relative importance of each of these three criteria in achieving the consumer strategy. The weights of the criteria under the other level 3 strategies similarly reflect their respective importance in achieving a particular strategy.

The next step in the AHP analysis is to evaluate the proposed projects with respect to the strategy criteria. With our relatively large number of projects (twelve), pairwise comparing the projects with respect to each of the relevant strategy criteria can become a bit challenging. Fortunately, we use the rating approach to complete this phase of the evaluation, shown as level 5 in Figure 2A.3. A rating scale can have as many categories as desired, but in our example we use five ratings for each criterion: *EXCELLENT, VERY GOOD, GOOD, FAIR,* and *NOT APPLICABLE.* The rating "NOT APPLICABLE" is used when a potential project (level 6) is judged to have no impact (i.e., provides no support) for a

CONSUMER STRATEGY CRITERIA (*CONSUMER*)
1. Overall ranking or perception by consumer of the firm relative to competitor firms (CONSRATE)
2. Customer service level of firm as judged by consumer based upon "product on-shelf availability" or similar measures (PRODAVL)
3. Capability of firm to assure that all targeted consumers have ready access to firm's goods and/or services (ACCESS)

CUSTOMER STRATEGY CRITERIA (*CUSTOMER*)
1. Overall ranking or perception of firm by customers relative to competitor firms (CUSTRATE)
2. Customer service level of firm as measured by item fill rate or similar measure (FILLRATE)
3. Customer's ranking or perception of supplier as potential long-run strategic partner (PARTNER)
4. Firm's capability to accurately segment its customers based upon individual customer's long-term growth and profitability potential (CUSTSEG)
5. Firm's capability to offer its customers leading edge customer relationship management services including IT, internet and related support (CRM)

GOVERNMENT & SOCIETAL STRATEGY CRITERIA (*GOV'T/SOCIETAL*)
1. Compliance level with all federal, state and local government environmental laws (ENVIRON)
2. Compliance level with all applicable governmental security and regulatory laws and agencies such as Homeland Security, OSHA, and FDA (SEC_REG)
3. Perception of the firm (relative to its peer firms) by the local and global communities where the firm does business (RELATION)
4. Capability of the firm to influence pertinent local or federal governments toward the firm's point of view on key policies and legislation that will affect the firm (INFLUENC)

FINANCIAL STRATEGY CRITERIA (*FINANCIAL*)
1. Cost competitiveness of firm's supply chain relative to the firm's direct competitors (COST_DIR)
2. Cost competitiveness of firm's supply chain relative to all firms in related industries (COST_IND)
3. Return on investment of supply chain projects (SCROI)
4. Productivity of firm's investment in inventory (INVENTRY)
5. Cash flow (i.e., order-to-cash cycle) generated by outbound logistics and customer service operations (CASHFLOW)

SUPPLIER & PARTNER STRATEGY CRITERIA (*SUPPLIER/PARTNER*)
1. Overall reliability of the firm's suppliers (RELIABL)
2. Overall quality of materials, components and other supplies furnished by firm's suppliers (QUALITY)
3. Flexibility and lead-time requirements of the firm's suppliers to respond to significant changes in supply requirements (FLEXIBIL)
4. Capability of firm to identify need for and maintain long-term partnership relationships with key suppliers (PARTNERS)
5. Cost competitiveness of firm's suppliers (COSTCOMP)

Figure 2A.4. AHP level 4—supply chain strategy criteria.—
(Continued)

INTERNAL STRATEGY CRITERIA (*INTERNAL*)
1. Capability of firm's supply chain to support the firm's business, marketing, and sales objectives (SCCAPABL)
2. Capability of firm's non-IT technology (e.g., manufacturing and warehousing technology) to support efficient and effective supply chain operations (NONITTEC)
3. Capability of firm's supply chain IT technology to support efficient and effective operations (ITTEC)
4. Quality of collective skill set levels of firm's supply chain employees to support current and future supply chain operations and management requirements (SKILLSET)
5. Productivity levels of firm's supply chain employees (PRODIVTY)

Figure 2A.4. AHP level 4—supply chain strategy criteria.

particular criterion (level 4). If a project does not support a specific strategy, then its rating is "NOT APPLICABLE" with respect to ALL criteria that support that strategy.

Figure 2A.5 illustrates the ratings scales for the CUSTOMER strategy. For example, an Excellent rating for FILLRATE requires that the project being evaluated will move Zenith's line item fill rate to customers to 99% or higher from its current 95% level. The four strategy areas not shown (i.e., CONSUMER, GOV'T/SOCIETAL, SUPPLIER/PARTNER, FINANCIAL, and INTERNAL) would have similar rating scales for each of their respective criteria. As shown in Figure 2A.5, the definitions of the rating scales are specific to the criteria being considered. These ratings can be pairwise compared for each criterion to establish their weights. For example, the AHP question might be: "When considering the Customer (CUST) strategy, how much better is an EXCELLENT rating than a VERY GOOD rating? Alternatively, the rating weights can be directly specified. In our example, the weights used for EXCELLENT, VERY GOOD, GOOD, FAIR, and NOT APPLICABLE for all criteria are 1.00, 0.65, 0.40, 0.15, and 0, respectively (level 5 in Figure 2A.3).[15]

The twelve projects that Zenith's supply chain organization has identified as candidates to support its strategies and objectives are shown as level 6 in Figure 2A.3. To simplify the discussion, we assume that each project supports only one strategy, as shown in Figure 2A.6. For example, Project 2, "Integrate POS (point of sale) Data as Input to Current Forecasting and Production Scheduling Processes" supports the CUSTOMER strategy, and so should only be rated on the criteria associated with this

Criterion: CUSTRATE

Rating	Definition
Excellent	Project will move firm from its current top 15% of all firms ranking to a top 5% ranking
Very Good	Project will move firm to top 10% ranking
Good	Project will move firm to top 13% ranking
Fair	Project will assure at least maintaining firm's current top 15% ranking
Not Applicable	Project does not support or affect this criterion

Criterion: FILLRATE

Rating	Definition
Excellent	Project will move firm's line item fill rate to customers to 99% or higher from its current 95% level
Very Good	Project will move firm to between 98% and 99% fill rate
Good	Project will move firm to between 96% and 98% fill rate
Fair	Project will move firm to between 95% and 96% fill rate
Not Applicable	Project does not support or affect this criterion

Criterion: PARTNER

Rating	Definition
Excellent	Project will allow the firm to improve its ranking to the top 5% (from its current top 20%) of all suppliers as customers' choice of a supplier with whom to form a long-term strategic partnership
Very Good	Project will assure that firm ranks in the top 8% of all suppliers as customers' choice for partnership
Good	Project will assure that firm ranks in the top 10% of all suppliers as customers' choice for partnership
Fair	Project will assure that firm ranks in the top 15% of all suppliers as customers' choice for partnership
Not Applicable	Project does not support or affect this criterion

Criterion: CUSTSEG

Rating	Definition
Excellent	Project will assure that firm can regularly update activity-based costing profit and loss (P&L) analyses and cost-to-serve rankings for its entire customer base; firm can classify all customers in a "strategic importance" quadrant analysis, and has organizational alignment on these rankings (e.g., alignment between sales, marketing and supply chain organizations). [Note firm currently only evaluates its profitability at an aggregate, corporate level and not at the customer level.]
Very Good	Project will assure that firm can perform annual P&L and cost-to-serve analyses of all customers
Good	Project will assure that firm can rank its customers based upon their annual sales, the average freight cost per lb to deliver products to each customer, and the overall profitability of each customer
Fair	Project will assure that firm can rank its customers based on their annual sales and the average freight cost per lb to deliver products to each customer
Not Applicable	Project does not support or affect this criterion

Figure 2A.5. Examples of ratings scale descriptions for criteria supporting the customer supply chain strategy.—(Continued)

Criterion: CRM	
Rating	*Definition*
Excellent	Project will make it possible for the firm to offer a comprehensive set of customer relationship management services to all eligible customers and to implement state of the art CRM internal IT and internet systems. [The firm currently has no significant CRM services.]
Very Good	Project will position the firm to offer selected customers a variety of CRM services backed by significant internal IT and internet systems
Good	Project will allow the firm to offer a few CRM services and develop moderate internal resources sufficient to serve a limited portion of customers who could qualify for CRM support
Fair	Project will position the firm to offer limited CRM services
Not Applicable	Project does not support or affect this criterion

Figure 2A.5. Examples of ratings scale descriptions for criteria supporting the customer supply chain strategy.

strategy. Therefore, the strategic planning team would evaluate this project based upon the rating scales of each of the five criteria defined under the CUSTOMER strategy. The specific ratings for all projects are also included in Figure 2A.6.

We are now ready to determine how well each of the projects supports the supply chain mission. Using project 2 as an example: (1) we convert its FILLRATE criterion rating of "Very Good" into 0.650; (2) multiply 0.650 by 0.173, FILLRATE's weight to yield the portion of the criterion weight earned (0.112); and (3) then multiply this result by 0.124, the CUST strategy weight to yield the portion of the strategy weight earned (0.014), as illustrated in Table 2A.1. Similar calculations are made for each criterion of the CUST strategy, and after summing the results over all criteria the result is a final score of 0.027 for Project 2. Figure 2A.7 provides a Decision Lens screen shot depicting the scoring of project 2 across the CUST criteria.

A similar approach is used to compute the scores for all projects, with the results shown in Table 2A.2. Additionally, this table also includes Zenith's estimated cost of completing each project, and the strategy that each project supports. At this point the supply chain team would be ready to make its final project selection decisions. One other key variable typically required would be the total budget or budget range available to the supply chain planning team. Using the summary information from Table 2A.2, and illustrative assumptions regarding

	Project description	Strategy project supports	Ratings for criteria of strategy each project supports
1	Streamline existing direct to consumer delivery and internet ordering services	CONS	consrate = E, prodavl = VG, access = VG
2	Integrate POS (point of sale) data as input to current forecasting and production scheduling processes	CUST	custrate = F, fillrate = VG, partner = F, custseg = NA, crm = NA
3	Establish and enhance customer relationship management services (CRM)	CUST	custrate = VG, fillrate = G, partner = E, custseg = G, crm = E
4	Implement a customer segmentation program based on customer profitability & activity based costing (ABC) analyses	CUST	custrate = G, fillrate = F, partner = VG, custseg = E, crm = F
5	Expand supplier relationship management programs	S&P	reliable = E, quality = VG, flexible = VG, partners = G, costcomp = G
6	Evaluate and benchmark current security processes and procedures on supply chain, and recommend enhancements	G&S	environ = NA, sec_reg = E, relation = VG, influenc = F
7	Integrate current individual country sales & operations planning processes into one global S&OP process	OPS&E	sccapabl = VG, nonittec = NA, ittec = G, skillset = G, prodivty = VG
8	Develop and implement plan to optimize use of RFID in supply chain and use of RFID vs. use of bar codes	OPS&E	sccapabl = F, nonittec = F, ittec = VG, skillset = NA, prodivty = VG
9	Evaluate current use of third party logistics (3PL) and recommend if firm should increase use of 3PLs	FIN	cost_dir = G, cost_ind = G, scroi = VG, inventry = F, cashflow = F
10	Develop and implement labor productivity measurement systems for plant and warehouse operations	OPS&E	sccapabl = VG, nonittec = G, ittec = VG, skillset = F, prodivty = E
11	Expand current import/export compliance IT capabilities	G&S	environ = NA, sec_reg = E, relation = G, influenc = F
12	Benchmark firm's current carbon footprint and develop long-termgreen manufacturing operations plan	G&S	environ = G, sec_reg = NA, relation = VG, influenc = G

Figure 2A.6. Zenith's potential supply chain project list.

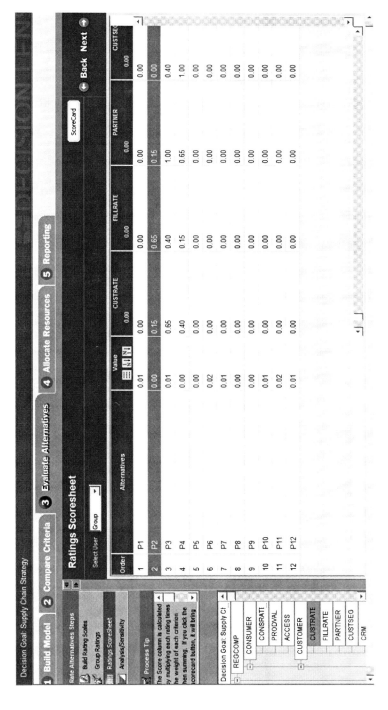

Figure 2A.7. Decision lens screen shot: entering project 2's scores for customer criteria.

Table 2A.1. "Project Score" Calculations for Project 2

Criterion	Cust strategy weight	Criterion weight	Rating contribution	Score
CUSTRATE	0.124	0.401	0.150 (Fair)	0.007
FILLRATE	0.124	0.173	0.650 (Very Good)	0.014
PARTNER	0.124	0.275	0.150 (Fair)	0.005
CUSTSEG	0.124	0.065	0.000 (NA)	0.000
CRM	0.124	0.086	0.000 (NA)	0.000
		Project 2 Total Score		0.026

Table 2A.2. Summary of Project Scores and Estimated Project Costs

Project	AHP project score	Estimated project cost ($ millions)	Strategy project supports
P1	0.059	$1.1	CONS
P2	0.027	$1.0	CUST
P3	0.078	$1.5	CUST
P4	0.053	$0.5	CUST
P5	0.039	$0.5	S&P
P6	0.236	$0.3	G&S
P7	0.177	$0.7	OPS&E
P8	0.038	$0.4	OPS&E
P9	0.064	$0.3	FIN
P10	0.103	$0.8	OPS&E
P11	0.222	$1.0	G&S
P12	0.089	$0.9	G&S

Zenith's budget constraints, we now describe a method to select the supply chain projects.

Projects are selected for funding based on their project scores, costs, and budget available. A project's benefit can be thought of as its AHP score, and so a benefit-cost ratio can be computed for each project. One approach is to fund projects in descending order of their benefit-cost ratio until the available funding resources are depleted. For example, project 6 has the highest benefit—cost ratio of 0.787 (0.236/0.30), and so it would be the first project funded, followed by project 7, whose

Table 2A.3. Projects Funded by Budget Level and Total Benefit Achieved

Project Cost $ (millions) / Zenith's Budget $ (millions) → Benefit: Total Score of Projects Selected →	$2.5 0.688	$3.0 0.727	$3.5 0.840	$4.0 0.893	$4.5 0.944	$5.0 0.983	$5.5 1.021	$6.0 1.041	$6.5 1.080	$7.0 1.099	$7.5 1.107
P1 ($1.1)									■		■
P2 ($1.0)											■
P3 ($1.5)										■	
P4 ($0.5)	■	■	■	■	■	■	■	■	■	■	■
P5 ($0.5)	■	■	■	■	■	■	■	■	■	■	■
P6 ($0.3)	■	■	■	■	■	■	■	■	■	■	■
P7 ($0.7)	■	■	■	■	■	■	■	■	■	■	■
P8 ($0.4)			■	■	■	■	■	■	■	■	■
P9 ($0.3)	■	■	■	■	■	■	■		■	■	■
P10 ($0.8)			■	■	■	■	■	■	■	■	■
P11 ($1.0)	■	■						■	■	■	■
P12 ($0.9)		■	■	■	■	■	■	■	■	■	■

■ = project is funded.

ratio is 0.253 (0.177/0.70). Therefore, if we had a $1 million dollar budget, we would fund these two projects to achieve a total benefit of 0.236 + 0.177 = 0.413. The benefit-cost approach works reasonably well, but doesn't always result in the set of projects that maximizes the total benefit across projects while staying within the budget. Decision support software such as *Decision Lens* uses a mathematical algorithm that achieves this purpose.[16] Table 2A.3 provides the scores and costs for each project, and indicates the set of projects that would be selected for funding based on different available budgets, a form of sensitivity analysis. For example, if the budget were $3.0 M, then projects 4, 5, 6, 7, and 11 would be funded, and the total benefit achieved in meeting the supply chain mission would be 0.727. Using this approach, the planning team could also employ additional constraints such as a requirement that at least one project supporting each strategy must be selected. Such changes are easily handled by the software.

Summary

The AHP approach facilitates direct linkages between the supply chain's mission, objectives, and strategies and the projects needed to execute the chosen strategies. It requires the planning team to make explicit judgments about the various factors that comprise the planning framework, as expressed in the form of pairwise comparisons. These judgments lead to weights for the objectives and strategies that determine their importance in achieving the mission. The proposed projects are evaluated by the extent to which they achieve criteria that are directly linked to specific supply chain strategies. The resulting project scores represent the sum total of the project's benefits in achieving the mission and can be combined with budget information to determine the set of projects to be funded. The planning framework and pairwise comparisons described can be entered and processed with a user-friendly AHP software package such as *Decision Lens Suite*.

CHAPTER 3

Hierarchical Supply Chain Planning and Scheduling Frameworks

Introduction

Hierarchical supply chain planning and scheduling frameworks can address an extremely broad range of planning and management activities ranging from scheduling a single plant to planning and scheduling operations over an entire global supply chain. Further, one can apply a hierarchical planning approach to any supply chain function ranging from procurement to transportation to inventory management. In this chapter, we introduce hierarchical planning by first reviewing a general rationale for this type of planning framework. Next, we review a generic framework for a hierarchical supply chain planning (HSCP) system. This will serve to clarify our definition of a HSCP framework. To further our understanding of this approach, we then review a case study of a firm that significantly reduced its annual operating costs and improved its customer service levels by implementing a HSCP to manage and schedule manufacturing and distribution operations over a multiechelon network. This case study highlights the benefits of integrated operations planning and scheduling over multiple functions.

In the second half of this chapter, we illustrate how individual functions of a supply chain can successfully utilize a hierarchical planning framework. Specifically, we demonstrate hierarchical planning approaches to organize the individual activities of inventory management and warehouse operations. The successful implementation of a HSCP system also requires the development of what we term "feedback loops" from lower to higher planning levels (e.g., from the operational level to the tactical level). We discuss feedback loops throughout the chapter, and then offer a tangible production planning example of a feedback loop in an appendix to Chapter 3.[1]

Rationale for Hierarchical Planning Frameworks

The introduction in Chapter 1 of a hierarchical planning framework with three broad planning categories both invites and answers the question of why hierarchical planning approaches first developed. Each of the three planning levels (the strategic, tactical, and operational) address a complex set of linked, but different decisions. These decisions differ across many dimensions including length of planning horizon, level of detail required of planning decision support data, risks and costs of the decisions, and long term impact of the decisions to name only a few. Now let's evaluate the implications of the markedly different characteristics of the decisions required at each level from several different perspectives.

From a managerial perspective, the broad dimensions of production planning and scheduling decisions virtually necessitate that multiple layers of management participate in the decision-making process. Senior management typically dominates the decision-making process at the strategic level, while less senior managers and supervisors generally assume the lead in tactical and operational decisions. Given this broad level of required management participation (i.e., hierarchy), it seems logical that a hierarchical decision making framework, decision support tools, and performance metrics would exist to facilitate the management process. Thus, when viewed from both a management perspective and a decision support or planning systems perspective, the breadth of activities associated with production planning, or any other supply chain function, demands a hierarchical approach.

The varying degrees of uncertainty and detail found in different decisions illustrate yet another key motive for developing a hierarchical planning framework. Strategic decisions require a highly aggregated level of information and they can influence a firm for many years into the future. In fact, the gestation period before the full impact of a strategic decision comes to bear often spans several years (e.g., the decision to build a new plant). On the other hand, operational decisions require very detailed data and can impact a firm within hours or days (e.g., the decision of what products to produce on a production line next week). Obviously therefore, managers must make different types of decisions at different points in time. It would not make sense to decide whether to produce a blue or a red widget on a production line in a particular week three years from today. It is far too uncertain today to predict what color widget will be required on a particular week in three years. Further, the lead time required to implement this decision is probably only a few hours or days, and thus the firm can postpone this decision until the last minute. In contrast, it most certainly makes sense to decide today what type of plant with what production capabilities should be built, if a firm has concluded that it will need additional capacity within three years. Even though this decision may hold significant risk, the lead time of plant site selection and construction will dictate that the firm act far in advance. The preceding rather simple examples further illustrate that a firm or organization can best address the varying levels of risk, uncertainty, lead time, analysis, and detail found and required in different decisions, by structuring supply chain decisions in hierarchical planning frameworks.

A Generic Framework for a Hierarchical Supply Chain Planning System

Figure 3.1 re-displays the generic business and supply chain planning framework originally presented in Chapter 1.

In this section we will examine further how a hierarchical planning framework works at the individual supply chain function level. Thus, we will focus on the lower half of the framework depicted in Figure 3.1. For illustration purposes, we will present a typical generic framework for the manufacturing and distribution function of a supply chain organization. Note that often in practice each of these functions may have their own separate planning framework.

Figure 3.2 presents a hierarchical manufacturing and distribution planning framework. At this point in the planning process, business unit strategic plans have been developed and approved, as have the high level strategic plans of the overall supply chain organization (discussed in Chapter 2). Now the manufacturing and distribution functions

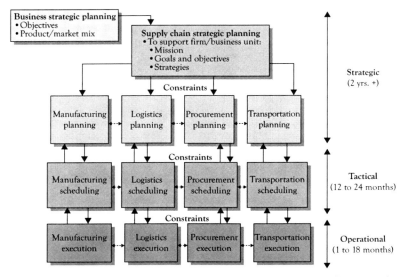

Figure 3.1. A unified business and supply chain planning framework.

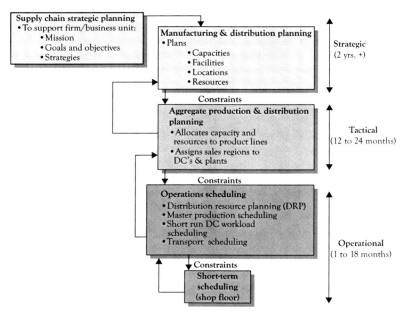

Figure 3.2. Hierarchical SC and manufacturing planning framework.

commence their own strategic planning processes to support the overall supply chain and business unit strategies.

At the strategic planning level, manufacturing must address such issues as planned production capacity levels for the next three years and beyond; the number of facilities it plans to operate, their locations, the resources it will assign to its manufacturing operations, and numerous other important long-term decisions. Similar decisions must be made for distribution facilities and resources. Decisions made at the strategic level place constraints on the tactical planning level. At the tactical level, typical planning activities include the allocation of capacity and resources to product lines for the next 12–18 months, aggregate planning of workforce levels, the development or fine-tuning of distribution plans, and numerous other activities. Within the constraints of the firm's manufacturing and distribution infrastructure (an infrastructure determined by previous strategic decisions), managers make tactical planning decisions designed to optimize the use of the existing infrastructure. Planning decisions carried out at the tactical level impose constraints upon operational planning and scheduling decisions. At this level, activities such as distribution resource planning (DRP), rough cut capacity planning, master production scheduling, shop floor control scheduling, and many other decisions occur.

As just described, a distinguishing characteristic of a hierarchical planning framework is that decisions made at higher planning levels (e.g., the strategic level) place constraints and boundaries on subsequent decisions that will later be made at lower planning levels (e.g., the tactical level). This facilitates aligned decision making across all levels of a supply chain organization and its individual functions from a "top down" perspective. To strengthen the alignment of organizational decision making, "hierarchical" planning frameworks also employ "feedback loops." Briefly, feedback loops represent both formal and informal mechanisms by which planners at lower levels of the planning hierarchy provide feedback to planners at higher levels. In Figure 3.2, the arrows flowing from the operational level to the tactical level, and from the tactical level to the strategic level, represent feedback loops.

Feedback loops are one of the most important characteristics of the hierarchical supply chain planning system illustrated in Figure 3.2. A true HSCP framework is a closed-loop system which employs a "top down"

complemented by "bottom up" feedback loops. Given
CP systems on evaluating capacity levels and impos-
communicating capacity constraints from higher levels down
⌣ ιower levels, it is imperative that strong feedback loops exist. As is well
known, production and distribution plans which appear feasible at an
aggregate level can often contain hidden infeasibilities that only manifest
themselves at lower, more disaggregated levels. (The Appendix at the end
of Chapter 3 will illustrate this issue.) Without proper feedback loops
imbedded into a hierarchical planning framework, the danger that a
supply chain function will attempt to move forward with infeasible plans
always exists. These infeasibilities often do not surface until an organization is in the midst of executing its operational plans and schedules.

The hierarchical framework presented in Figure 3.2 is generic in that
although individual HSCP systems will differ by supply chain function and
by firm, most systems are designed within this or a similar general framework.
Figure 3.3 recaps some illustrative generic decisions that a HSCP system
constructed within this framework will generally address and it displays
how these decisions fit into a planning hierarchy. As several of the illustrative decisions in Figure 3.3 imply, HSCP systems typically extend beyond a
firm's internal operations to include decisions about suppliers and customers.

Illustrative network issues and challenges

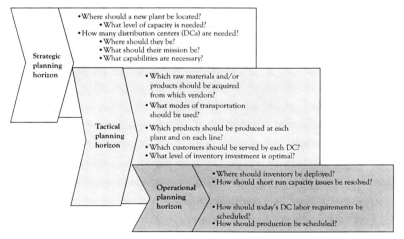

*Figure 3.3. Illustration: how network decisions fit into a planning
hierarchy.*

With a general framework in place, the next step in constructing a HSCP framework consists of designing its actual components. At this point it becomes more difficult to describe a "generic" HSCP system because actual implementations all possess unique characteristics reflective of the particular firm or industry where the HSCP framework is applied. For purposes of illustrating an actual implementation, we present a brief case study in the next section.

A Case Study of a Hierarchical Supply Chain Planning Framework Implementation

The case study of a hierarchical manufacturing and logistics planning framework presented in this section is originally based on an implementation which the authors led at American Olean Tile Company.[2] This general framework was later implemented at other firms (e.g., Pfizer/Warner-Lambert).[3] For purposes of this book, we will focus strictly on the HSCP framework developed over a period of several years at American Olean (AO). Readers interested in the full case study are referred to Miller (2002)[4] for a complete company and case description.

The American Olean Tile Company manufactured a wide variety of ceramic wall and floor tile products, and elaborate mural designs. The firm sold all of its products nationally, with the northeastern and southeastern states, and California accounting for the greatest portion of overall demand. At the time it implemented its HSCP system, AO operated eight factories located across the US from New York to California that supplied approximately 120 sales distribution points (SDPs) which consisted of a combination of sales territories and company-owned warehouses. Each manufacturing facility had a finished goods warehouse located adjacent to the plant. Figure 3.4 illustrates the AO network. These factories utilized several different production processes, all of which began with a crushing and milling procedure, and which eventually led to the firing of tile in large kilns. AO produced three basic lines of tile products: (1) glazed tile, (2) ceramic mosaics, and (3) quarry tile. The quarry division operated factories in four states (Pennsylvania, Alabama, Kentucky, and California), while the glazed and ceramic mosaic divisions each had two manufacturing sites, respectively.

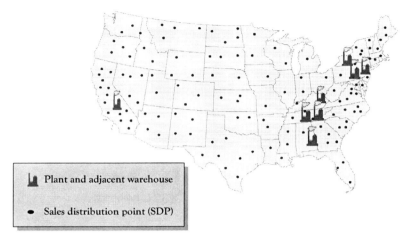

Figure 3.4. American Olean Tile manufacturing and distribution network.

As the firm's network grew, the lack of coordination which existed between manufacturing planning and distribution planning had become an increasingly significant problem for the firm. For example, AO frequently found itself unnecessarily shipping finished goods inventory back and forth between distribution centers because manufacturing and distribution planned their operations independently. This situation eventually prompted AO's management to sponsor a project to address this planning problem. Initially the program was chartered simply to integrate the annual production and distribution planning processes. However, shortly after the project began, it became clear that AO would not reap the full benefits from integrated annual plant, product and distribution assignments if it did not also assure that alignment existed between short-term scheduling and inventory control decisions, and annual plans. Thus, AO's management commissioned the development of a full-scale hierarchical production and distribution planning system. The objective of implementing this system was to improve the integration of annual production and distribution planning, short-term scheduling and inventory control.

The designers of American Olean's HSCP system implemented it with the intent that their system would support the firm's network-wide strategic, tactical, and operational planning activities. AO fully implemented its

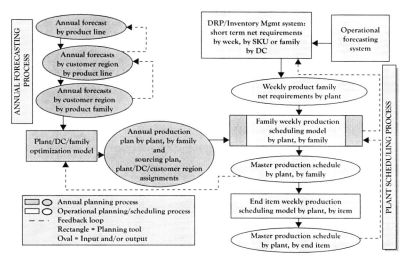

Figure 3.5. AO's hierarchical supply chain planning framework (tactical/annual planning and operational scheduling).

hierarchical supply chain planning framework in about two years, and Figure 3.5 depicts the completed system. This framework positioned AO to generate coordinated strategic, tactical, and operational plans and schedules. We will now briefly review the components of this system, focusing first on tactical and operational planning and scheduling. After this we will address how this framework also facilitated strategic planning.

Because annual and 18-month rolling planning horizons represent the most common tactical planning horizons, we illustrate an integrated annual and operational planning and scheduling system. Note that the dark shaded boxes and ovals in Figure 3.5 indicate elements of the annual planning process, while the other boxes and ovals constitute the operational planning and scheduling process.

Tactical (Annual) Planning Process

The process commences with the development of annual or 12–18 month rolling forecasts by major product line. For this example, we assume a product hierarchy consisting from top to bottom of (1) major product line, (2) product family, and (3) end item where product families represent aggregations of similar end items, and product lines represent aggregations of similar product families. Techniques used to generate forecasts at this level vary widely and include econometric forecasting, exponential smoothing[5] time series-based forecasting methods and so on. Importantly, exogenous market intelligence and sales judgment factors often provide critical inputs at this level. Thus, a firm's ability to structure a process, which effectively integrates quantitative techniques and qualitative inputs, represents a key determinant of the accuracy of major product line forecasts.

The next step consists of disaggregating product line forecasts into product line forecasts by customer region. Methodologies for generating these lower level product line forecasts again vary widely and range from simple techniques such as using recent historical ratios of each customer region's demand to total demand, to complex quantitative approaches[6]. The size of individual customer regions strongly influences the approach at this level. For example, in a global HSCP system, customer regions may represent geographic regions such as a country or a group of countries. Global applications tend to utilize more sophisticated methods to develop product line forecasts. In fact, some firms choose to develop global product line forecasts from aggregations of individual country product line forecasts. (Note the feedback loop between the product line forecast by customer region and the total product line forecast.) On the other hand, in an HSCP system covering a smaller geography (e.g., a domestic U.S. system) where customer regions represent relatively small entities (e.g., parts of individual states), it is more likely to observe simpler methods employed to disaggregate product line forecasts into product line forecasts by customer regions.

Next, customer region product line forecasts are disaggregated into product family forecasts by customer region. There is no universally correct approach for all forecasting applications and often several schemes will work well. One common approach is to use the recent historical percentage which each product family comprises of a customer region's total sales to disaggregate a customer region product line forecast into individual product family forecasts for the customer region. AO employed this methodology to identify and project regional variations in the demand for its different product families.

The product family forecasts by customer regions are important inputs for tactical/annual planning, and specifically for the plant/distribution center/product family optimization model. Linear and mixed integer programming optimization[7] models are the standard decision-support tools utilized for planning at the tactical/annual level. Annual optimization models most frequently define products at the product family level[8]. Further, assuming that the HSCP application involves multiple manufacturing or distribution locations, these annual optimization models define demand by appropriate geographic regions. Hence, the need for annual product family forecasts by customer region. If the annual model contains multiple time periods (e.g., months or quarters), then it requires the annual product family forecasts by customer region, by time period (i.e., one additional level of disaggregation). Figure 3.6 highlights some of the key outputs derived from the annual plant/DC/family (PDCF) optimization model.

As Figure 3.6 indicates, the annual optimization model creates a production plan by plant, by family, by time period and sourcing assignments by plant, by distribution center, by customer region.

As shown in Figure 3.5, the last major step of the annual planning process consists of evaluating the annual optimization model's production plans for each plant in a weekly production scheduling model. Briefly, this family weekly production scheduling model helps to determine whether the production plans developed for a plant by the annual model remain feasible when evaluated at a greater level of detail than possible in an annual model. Typical examples include evaluating production plans in weekly time buckets rather than in quarterly buckets or a single annual bucket, and evaluating the impact of weekly production changeovers on the feasibility of an annual production plan. The weekly production scheduling model produces a master production schedule

---

- **Distribution plan**
  - Assigns sales regions to DC's and plants (i.e., a sourcing plan)
  - Establishes plant to DC and inter-DC shipping (supply) plans
- **Annual production plan, for each plant, by time period**
  - Establishes planned operating rates for each plant (i.e., capacity utilization rates)
  - Assigns production product mixes for each plant (by defined product families)
- **Inventory plan for planning horizon, by time period**

Figure 3.6. Outputs from optimization model.

for a plant at the family level. It is not unusual to find that production plans which appeared feasible at the annual level manifest infeasibilities when evaluated at the weekly level. This results because annual integrated manufacturing/distribution models typically do not include changeover costs or setup times, nor do they define time buckets at weekly levels. Thus, in Figure 3.5, the feedback loop shown between the output of the weekly plant scheduling model and the annual optimization model represents a critical part of the annual planning process. Clearly, a firm must develop an annual production plan which each of its plants can feasibly implement at the operational level. The feedback loop from the weekly model to the annual model assures this. (See the Appendix to Chapter 3 for additional details.)

This completes the integrated annual hierarchical generic planning process. Next we briefly review the operational planning and scheduling process. Based upon the tactical (annual) planning process, sourcing patterns have been defined (e.g., what plant serves which DC and what DC serves which customer region). The operational planning and scheduling system executes these decisions on a day-to-day and week-to-week basis.

Operational Planning and Scheduling Process

Figure 3.5 illustrates a standard operational planning and scheduling system. A forecasting system, frequently time-series, exponential smoothing based, generates forecasts at the item or SKU level. These forecasts feed an inventory management system, often a DRP system, which generates net requirements by week, by SKU and/or by family for each distribution center. The DC's place their weekly net requirements upon their source plants and this creates the weekly net requirements by end item, by family for a manufacturing plant. These weekly net requirements drive the family weekly production scheduling model. Note that this short run focused scheduling model could be defined in different time buckets (e.g., days or two-week periods) if appropriate. Also, note that a feedback loop flows from the weekly scheduling model back to the inventory management module. Should the weekly scheduling model determine that a plant cannot meet the weekly family net requirements, this feedback loop communicates the infeasibility. An iterative process would then ensue whereby either the original net requirements are modified until a feasible plan can be produced, or excess production requirements are addressed by such options as overtime production or the offloading of some net requirements to other plants.

The final major step outlined in the generic process of Figure 3.5 is the plant's master production schedule by end item. The plant's weekly master production schedule by family provides the input which drives the end item scheduling model. This model produces a traditional master production schedule of end items by weekly time bucket. Note that a feedback loop also flows from the master production end item schedule back to the weekly family production scheduling model. This feedback loop is required because it is possible that a schedule which appears feasible at the weekly, family level may mask infeasibilities that become evident at the item level. This completes our discussion of the tactical and operational components of AO's HSCP framework, illustrated in Figure 3.5.[9]

The implementation of this framework and system reduced the firm's annual operating costs by about 10%. Additionally, it facilitated fully integrated tactical and short-run production and distribution plans and schedules, resulting in enhanced customer service levels and significantly reduced "unplanned" emergency interfacility inventory transfers.[10]

As described, this system is generic in that it is applicable to a wide range of industries and firms. Individual firms may use a subset or perhaps variations on all of the framework components reviewed. Some firms will have additional components not covered here. Regardless of the particular components employed by an individual firm, the key requirement remains that all of the modules of an HSCP system must be linked together in a coordinated, hierarchical approach, as AO's system illustrates.

We close this section by noting that for many firms, including AO, there exist many critical operational planning and scheduling activities that occur after (and often are driven by) end item schedules. Systems that generate schedules for components of the end item represent just one example. We will not attempt to address these activities, but rather simply recognize that many of these work-in-process and raw materials plans and schedules have hierarchical characteristics similar to those reviewed at the finished goods level.

Strategic Planning Support

The tactical and operational planning system of AO also supported the firm's strategic planning process. To understand how, consider Figure 3.5 and the following example. The tactical plant/DC/family (PDCF) optimization model contained the following data:

- The production costs, rates, capacities, and product mix capabilities of each production line at each plant, by product family
- The distribution center costs, rates, and capacities at each DC on AO's network, by product family
- The freight and related costs to transport product between each plant and each DC, and between each DC and each customer region on the network
- The forecast demand by product family for each customer region

AO's standard tactical business planning process required that its planning team update all the inputs to the PDCF model at least once every six months. This assured that the firm always had current data available on all the key manufacturing and distribution costs, rates, and capacities for its network at all times. For strategic planning purposes this represented an extremely important capability. For example, over time, it became clear that AO's distribution center storage and throughput capacity would have to expand to meet the firm's increasing demand. The availability and currency of the PDCF model and other tactical planning components such as the forecasting models positioned AO to rapidly generate powerful quantitative assessments of its network expansion options. Specifically, to support its strategic planning process, AO could easily modify its existing tactical PDCF models to include potential new DC locations to add to its network. This of course required that the firm develop estimates of the costs and capacities of potential new DCs. AO would then evaluate through its optimization models how each potential new location would impact the entire network, and what new location to pursue. Therefore, because AO updated ͇tical planning tools regularly, it could readily engage in strategic plan-͇ssments of its network at any time with relatively minimal notice.

Summary

This business process gave the firm a truly agile hierarchical planning capability. In addition to its standard operational and tactical planning process, it could launch into a strategic planning exercise very rapidly at any time should this be required. Additionally, the firm conducted a regularly scheduled strategic planning process annually. If AO had not devoted the time and resources necessary to maintain its robust tactical and operational planning frameworks, its strategic planning process would have similarly deteriorated. Finally, it is also important to recognize that the linkages between AO's strategic, tactical, and operational planning processes, facilitated by a well-defined hierarchical framework, assured aligned decision making in the manufacturing and distribution functions from top to bottom.

Applying Hierarchical Frameworks to Individual Supply Chain Functions

One can apply a hierarchical framework to virtually any major function within a supply chain. Transportation, inventory, demand management, manufacturing, and distribution (e.g., the AO implementation) represent just a few examples of major functional areas that can benefit from a hierarchical framework. In this section, we highlight the broad applicability of hierarchical approaches by presenting frameworks constructed for two individual supply chain functions: (1) warehouse operations, and (2) inventory management.

Warehouse Operations

The warehouse planning process begins at the network-wide strategic planning level. At this level, a firm must determine how warehouse operations fit into its overall strategic plan, and in particular, what is the mission of the warehouses on its network. Figure 3.7 provides a high level overview of this hierarchical planning process that begins at the strategic level.

A first step in the planning process consists of determining the mission of the overall warehouse network and the individual locations that will

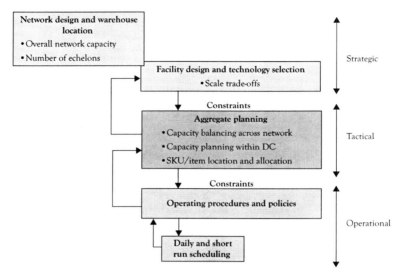

Figure 3.7. Hierarchical warehouse planning.

make up the network. Note that not all warehouses on a network will necessarily have the same mission or play the same role. The number of warehouse echelons to establish represents another common strategic network design question that heavily influences the mission of individual warehouses. For example, a firm must decide whether it will operate a single echelon network in which every warehouse will receive shipments of all products directly from all plants, or alternatively does the firm want to operate a multiechelon warehouse network where one or more first echelon, central warehouses receive products from plants and then redistribute some or all products to second echelon regional warehouses. Another important strategic decision concerns the question of whether a firm chooses to operate its own facilities or to outsource some or all of its warehouse operations to third party providers. Finally, as Figure 3.7 illustrates, total network warehouse capacity requirements and the economies of scale trade-offs are two additional key determinants of the interrelated decisions on network design, facility design, and warehouse technology selection.

At the tactical level, a firm must concern itself with such planning activities as balancing the demand for warehousing capacity across its network, and planning the most efficient and effective utilization of its capacity at each individual DC. Capacity planning at the individual DC level can involve determining the overall labor level and mix required to meet the projected demands over the planning horizon, the proper mix and use of available storage locations (e.g., type of racking where adjustable), and so on. In general, tactical warehouse planning focuses on the determination of how to best employ the existing network infrastructure (i.e., the existing warehouses and material handling equipment). Additionally, decisions to purchase relatively minor additional warehousing assets (e.g., incremental material handling equipment, racking, etc.) will occur in the tactical planning process. Major infrastructure issues that a firm cannot resolve at the tactical planning level (e.g., inadequate network capacity to meet forecast long term warehouse throughput or storage requirements) must typically be fed back up to the strategic planning level for resolution. Thus, the efficacy of hierarchical warehouse planning and scheduling relies upon feedback loops, similar, for example, to the dependency of effective production planning on such mechanisms.

At the operational level, a broad assortment of warehouse planning and scheduling activities take place on a regular basis. For example, the scheduling of labor and short-term assignments of items to storage locations represent two of the major operational planning activities. Typically, it is the nonroutine components of these activities (e.g., addressing temporary labor or storage requirements that significantly exceed capacity) that require the most critical attention. It is also typically the "exceptions" or "nonroutine" requirements of operational planning and scheduling that planners must report or "feed back" to the tactical planning level. For example, when warehouse planners consistently find themselves having to schedule "unplanned" outside storage because of insufficient facility storage capacity, they should send this information to the tactical level for resolution. Perhaps the overall warehouse network is out of balance and requires re-alignment because excess storage capacity exists at certain warehouses, while other warehouses face the opposite situation. Alternatively, perhaps this storage capacity issue at one warehouse is not an imbalance issue, but rather is occurring regularly across the network and requires a total network solution. This represents just one simple example of the types of feedback loops that must exist between the operational and tactical warehouse planning levels.

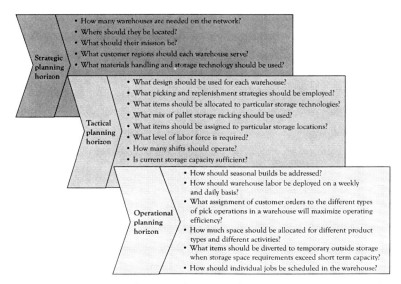

Figure 3.8. How warehousing decisions fit into a planning hierarchy.

We close this section with Figure 3.8 which displays a sample of the key decisions that warehouse network planners must tackle. Similar to other supply functions, the figure illustrates the breadth and depth of warehouse network issues that exist, hence the need for a hierarchical planning framework.

Inventory Management

Similar to production and distribution decisions, inventory decisions encompass all three levels of the planning hierarchy. Figure 3.9 offers an overview of where some key inventory decisions fit into a planning hierarchy. While this set of decisions does not represent a comprehensive list, it serves to illustrate how key inventory decisions span multiple planning horizons. For illustrative purposes, we now consider several of these decisions in more detail.

At the strategic planning level, inventory decisions revolve around such questions as what is the optimal level of inventory investment that a firm should plan to maintain on an ongoing basis. This decision requires an evaluation of a number of intertwined trade-offs. For example, in many cases manufacturing firms must consider what represents the best

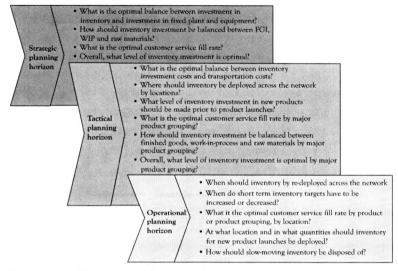

Figure 3.9. Hierarchical frameworks for individual supply chain functions: inventory management example.

mix of investment in manufacturing capacity vis-à-vis total investment in inventory. As a general rule, for any given level of network-wide demand, as a firm increases its manufacturing capacity and flexibility, it decreases the level of inventory investment that it must make. This is particularly the case for make-to-stock firms. For example, if a firm has the capacity and flexibility to produce its entire product line during one week (i.e., cycle through its full set of products), it will require less finished goods inventory to fill customer orders than if the firm requires several weeks or months to cycle through its product line. In general, the more heavily a firm chooses to invest in fixed plant and production equipment, the greater its production capacity and flexibility. Thus, at the strategic level, a manufacturer must decide the best balance to maintain between fixed assets and inventory investment.

The inventory investment decision also requires that a firm consider the trade-offs between relative levels of investment in finished goods inventory versus raw materials and work-in-process components. Additionally, at a very high level, a firm must develop a strategy on its planned customer service level fill rate. For example, a make-to-stock manufacturer cannot simply plan to have a 100% customer line fill rate.

This is not realistic. Thus, a manufacturer must put a service level strategy in place considering the trade-offs between some "acceptable" level of lost or unfulfilled demands versus the inventory investment associated with alternative service levels. Finally, such issues as the appropriate trade-off between transportation costs and inventory investment costs also require consideration in the inventory management process. Often manufacturers must choose between using faster, more expensive transport services (e.g., air) between a "supplying" origin and a "receiving" destination and slower, less expensive transportation alternatives. A key question in such decisions is do the savings in inventory investment requirements (i.e., in-transit and safety stock inventory at the destination) facilitated by a faster replenishment transit time with less variability outweigh the increased costs of the expedited transport service. Questions such as this often represent tactical rather than strategic issues; however, they play a prominent role in a firm's overall inventory investment approach.

At the tactical planning level, many of the same inventory issues found at the strategic level re-surface, but at a greater level of granularity. For example, typically a firm's annual planning process includes an evaluation of the level of the total inventory investment that it will make during the next year. At the minimum, however, this process will usually include an analysis at the major product grouping (e.g., brand or product family) level. In contrast the strategic inventory planning process will not address this level of detail. Many of the same trade-offs considered at the strategic level again re-appear in more detail (e.g., evaluating optimal service level fill rates and the appropriate mix of finished, in-process and raw materials inventory at the product grouping level). Further, as previously noted, decisions implemented at the strategic level will impact options at the tactical level. For example, the manufacturing capacity and flexibility built into the firm's current infrastructure will heavily influence its annual inventory investment plan.

At the tactical level other more detailed decisions such as the deployment of inventory by location and by product grouping will also occur for the first time. An example of the type of feedback that can develop at this level would be if a firm's planners, when reviewing inventory requirements by major product grouping, determine that in order to meet planned service fill rates, they require a total inventory level exceeding the planned overall investment target. Additionally, at this level, specific policies must be developed covering such potential issues as whether certain customers will receive priority in the event of temporary inventory shortages during the planning horizon. The development of guidelines for when inventory should be re-deployed between locations on a firm's network because of shortages and/or imbalances represents another example of the types of policies developed at the tactical planning level.

At the operational planning and execution level, again many previous planning decisions made at higher levels are revisited at a more detailed product line level and in more detailed time increments. Here a firm's planners must ensure that all SKUs (i.e., items at unique locations) have inventory targets designed to deliver specific customer service fill rates. Additionally, decisions regarding inventory targets by season, by month (perhaps even by week) must be made, and made within the guidelines or constraints established at higher planning levels. Inventory policies represent a common area where the existence of good feedback loops from the operational level to the tactical level can play an important role. If for example the guidelines regarding inventory re-deployment between network locations in cases of inventory imbalances are not working effectively, this information must be communicated back to the tactical planning level so that a more effective approach can be developed and implemented.

In summary, the inventory management function shares the same critical need for coordination and feedback between hierarchical planning levels as do the manufacturing and distribution functions, and all other individual supply chain functions.

Conclusion: Benefits

In closing this chapter, we now consider additional benefits of the framework approach. A firm that actively employs frameworks for its supply chain functions can rapidly evaluate whether potential new processes or decision support tools (e.g., scheduling software) can enhance the efficiency of its supply chain. Specifically, through its frameworks a firm's management understands how its current supply chain activities interface with each other at the operational, tactical, and strategic level, as well across these levels. When considering a potential addition or revision to its supply chain, the firm's decision makers evaluate how the proposed change fits into its existing framework. What are the new interfaces and communications that would be required? Does the proposed addition or revision really just duplicate a capability that already exists, or does it truly improve a function or process? These represent the types of important questions to which well-maintained frameworks facilitate insightful, broad-based answers. In the absence of frameworks, firms have a greater risk of making more "one-off," ineffective supply chain decisions.

Further, maintaining good frameworks of each major function can accelerate the assimilation of new tools and methodologies into a function. Once managers decide to introduce a new methodology or decision-support tool, the perspective provided by their frameworks of the supply chain functions allows them to best leverage the utility of the new capability. In summary, the practice of maintaining good frameworks of a firm's major supply chain functions represents a valuable and potentially "differentiating" capability to assure an efficient and effective supply chain.

Appendix 3A: Illustration of a Feedback Loop from the Operational Level to the Tactical Level

Feedback loops from the operational level to the tactical level and from the tactical level to the strategic level represent a "key and defining attribute" of any HSCP system. To provide additional perspective of what a feedback loop is, in this appendix we review an illustrative feedback loop from the Family Weekly Production Scheduling model to the Plant/DC/Family (PDCF) model in Figure 3.5.[11]

As previously discussed, in the tactical planning process, the PDCF model generates a 12–18 month production plan at the product family level for each plant in a network. The model also creates an integrated distribution plan that identifies which plants supply which DCs, and which DCs serve which customers, again at the product family level. Figure 3A.1 displays a network-wide annual production plan that for illustrative purposes we will assume the PDCF model has created. This plan displays the weeks of production of each product family that each

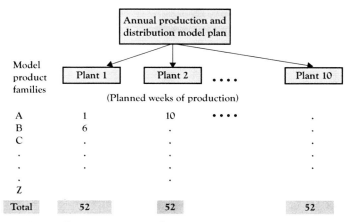

Figure 3A.1. Illustrative tactical production plan created by the plant/DC/family optimization model.

plant will manufacture over a 12-month planning horizon. (For simplicity the figure primarily shows "dots" rather than all 26 product families and their assignments.)

For illustration we now focus on the PDCF model's assignment that Plant 1 should produce one week of product family A. We will also assume that product family A has the following attributes:

1. It contains 20 finished good end items, and
2. Each of the 20 end items has a minimum production run length of a 1/2 day (i.e., if the plant has to produce an item, it must produce the item for a minimum of 1/2 of a day).

Briefly end items are aggregated into product families for tactical planning based upon their respective similar characteristics. For example, assume that this is a ceramic tile manufacturing network such as AOs, and that the 20 end items in product family A are different color 2″ × 2″ wall tile end items (e.g., blue, green, yellow, etc.). Each end item can be produced on the same production lines at the same plants, and at very similar costs per unit and at similar output rates. These similar end items would be planned as one product family in the PDCF model at the tactical planning level.

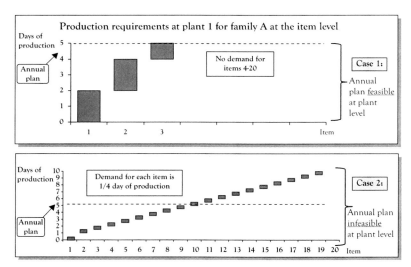

Figure 3A.2. Two scenarios for product family A at plant 1.

Now let's consider Figure 3A.2 which depicts two very different scenarios (Case 1 and Case 2), under which the PDCF model could generate an initial assignment of one week of production for product family A at plant 1. The total demand for product family A consists of the sum of the demand for the 20 end items that comprise this product family. (For simplicity we will also define production requirements as equal to total demand in this example.) Now consider Case 1 and Case 2 in Figure 3A.2.

- *Case 1:* The total demand (and production requirements) for
  product family A at plant 1 is in three end items (1, 2, and 3).
  - There is no demand for end items 4 through 20
    (i.e., demand = 0)
  - Thus, as Figure 3A.2 depicts, to satisfy the demand
    for product family A at plant 1 will require two days
    production of item 1, two days of item 2 and one day of
    item 3. No production of items 4 through 20 is required.
  - Therefore, plant 1 can feasibly produce the production
    assignment from the PDCF model of one week of family A.
    (Note that we define five business days as one week in this
    example.)

- *Case 2:* The total demand for product family A at plant 1 consists of ¼ of a day's production for each of its twenty end items.
  - 20 × 1/4 = 5 business days total demand; or one week of demand (and production)—the assignment of the PDCF model to plant 1 for family A.
  - Recall however that plant 1 has a minimum production run length of 1/2 day for any item.
  - Therefore, for plant 1 to produce all twenty items in family A will require 20 × 1/2 = 10 business days of production.
  - Thus, the production assignment from the PDCF model to plant 1 for product family A is not feasible.

How Can This Infeasible Production Assignment Occur

At the network-wide tactical planning level, models and planners generally do not evaluate very detailed issues such as the minimum run length of individual end items at individual plants. The purpose and objectives of 12–18 months planning exercises at the tactical level necessitate that planning/modeling be conducted at more aggregated levels (e.g., product families rather than end items). This allows the possibility that plans developed at the tactical level may in some cases be infeasible to implement at the operational level. Case 2 illustrates how these infeasibilities may arise.

In practice, "feedback loops" from lower planning and scheduling levels to higher levels take on great importance because of the type of situation illustrated in Case 2. As plans cascade down from one level to the next lower level (e.g., network-wide to individual plant), managers at the lower level must evaluate these plans and communicate back any infeasibilities. This becomes an iterative process whereby tactical plans should be revised based on feedback loop communications, and then revised tactical plans are re-evaluated at the operational level. This process continues until a feasible plan, at all levels, has been developed. The reader is referred to Miller (2002)[12] for additional discussion of feedback loops and hierarchical systems.

CHAPTER 4

Decision Support Frameworks and Methods for Effective Supply Chain Management

Introduction

In Chapters 1 through 3, we reviewed the value of using frameworks for supply chain management, explored the importance of integrated business and supply chain planning, and examined the hierarchical characteristics of supply chain management frameworks. We also presented a framework for overall supply chain strategic planning and illustrated how individual supply chain functions such as manufacturing can manage their activities through hierarchical planning frameworks. As introduced in Chapter 1, however, while a firm's supply chain organization needs to organize and conduct its planning activities through frameworks, effective supply chain management also requires strong *decision support systems* to facilitate all planning and management actions.

Decision support systems (DSS) are required at each level of a supply chain planning horizon (i.e., the strategic, tactical, and operational). Figure 4.1, first presented in Chapter 1, illustrates this support role that a DSS must play.

In this chapter, using a series of case study examples, we illustrate the importance and power of DSS. We begin with a brief introduction of what DSS are, and their value to a supply chain organization. Next we discuss the importance of integrating the components of a DSS across the strategic, tactical, and operational levels. We then examine a case study of a DSS developed by a firm over several years to support all planning

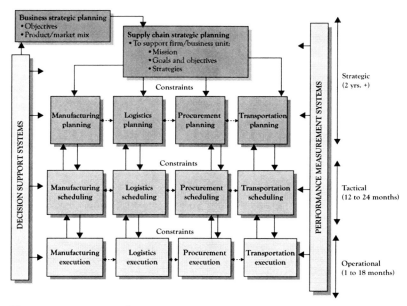

Figure 4.1. DSS and PMS integration into business and SC planning framework.

activities from the short run operational to the long run strategic. A second case study of a strategic and tactical manufacturing optimization planning DSS then follows, and we conclude with a case study of an operational daily inventory deployment DSS. This latter case will also illustrate how a supply chain DSS should be directly linked to a firm's ERP (Enterprise Resource Planning) system. Across all three cases, we will observe how strong DSS contributed to improved customer service levels and cost savings or revenue enhancements.

Supply Chain Decision Support Systems

Supply chain DSS represent a very broad category of tools and methodologies ranging from mathematical optimization algorithms to large-scale information technology data warehouses. There are at least two basic requirements of a supply chain DSS: (1) the appropriate data for a planning analysis must be available, and (2) the appropriate planning tool to perform the analysis must also be available. Finally, and just as

Supply chain DSS tools
■ Network optimization models
■ Network simulation models
■ Forecasting models (summary and detailed)
■ Inventory management (DRP) models
■ Plant scheduling models (Product Family–higher level)
■ Plant scheduling models (MPS–item level)
■ Warehouse (DC) capacity models (high level)
■ Warehouse (DC) short-run scheduling models
■ Transportation scheduling models

Figure 4.2. Illustrative supply chain decision support tools.

critical, a supply chain organization must have talented planners with the requisite skill sets to utilize the firm's data and analytic tools.[1] For our purposes, we define a supply chain DSS as any combination of data and analytic tools that facilitate strategic, tactical and operational planning and scheduling. To clarify what we mean by supply chain DSS, Figure 4.2 displays a sample of typical supply chain decision support tools.

The models listed in Figure 4.2 include several traditional DSS tools frequently used for manufacturing and distribution planning. For example, the American Olean Tile Company hierarchical planning framework reviewed in Chapter 3 employed many of these tools (see Figure 3.4). These models range from methodologies that support strategic planning such as network optimization, to techniques that address operational planning needs such as warehouse short run scheduling. This highlights a critical requirement of a DSS. A firm's supply chain DSS must address all of its planning requirements from the very long run to the short run day-to-day. Whether a firm is in the initial stages of constructing its DSS, or if it is expanding a mature system's capabilities, the ability of a DSS to support the full planning horizon represents a critical consideration. A firm that has excellent *strategic* planning tools but poor *operational* planning tools will struggle with execution. Conversely, a firm with strong *operational* tools but weak *strategic* tools will experience inefficiencies in its supply chain operations caused by such issues as inadequate long run infrastructure planning.

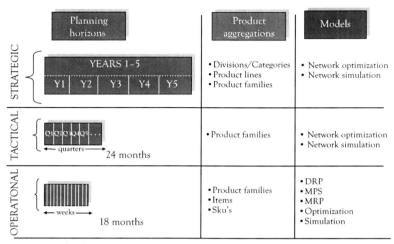

DRP = distribution requirements planning, MPS = master production scheduling,
MRP = material requirements planning

Figure 4.3. Planning horizons, product aggregations, and models for hierarchical planning.

Thus, a comprehensive supply chain DSS supports all three planning horizons. Figure 4.3 provides a perspective on the planning horizons, product aggregations, and types of models found in a hierarchical DSS.

Notice that the three planning horizons differ not only in timeframe, but also in granularity. While operational planning time buckets range from weeks and months down to hours and shifts, strategic planning time buckets are more typically defined in years or often in one time bucket (e.g., a plan for the next 3–5 years viewed as one bucket). In terms of product aggregations, again the planning hierarchy flows from the highly granular at the operational level (e.g., end items) to the highly aggregated at the strategic level (e.g., an entire division or business unit's products). In terms of DSS tools, there are some such as distribution requirements planning (DRP) or master production scheduling (MPS) which generally support only operational planning and scheduling.[2] On the other hand, there are some DSS tools such as mathematical optimization and simulation that can facilitate strategic, tactical and operational planning and scheduling. As one would expect, the actual planning tools which employ a specific methodology differ dramatically for each time horizon. For example, mathematical optimization algorithms power software used to evaluate large-scale global manufacturing and distribution networks (*strategic planning*), and similarly power software utilized for single production line scheduling at individual plants (*operational planning*).

Aligning DSS Across the Strategic, Tactical, and Operational Levels

To assure that a DSS will effectively serve the planning needs of a supply chain organization, a firm must construct a comprehensive system that is integrated and aligned across the three planning horizons. What does this really mean? To address this question, we first return to Figure 4.3 for a brief illustration. Then we review a case study of a logistics organization that developed a large-scale DSS over several years to support its operational through strategic planning and analytic requirements.

Figure 4.3 illustrates that techniques such as mathematical optimization can serve planning needs at all three planning levels. For example, in Chapter 3 we observed that American Olean Tile (see Figure 3.4) utilized manufacturing and distribution network models to:

1. Plan the optimal location and size of new plants or DCs (strategic planning),
2. Generate annual production and distribution plans for each plant and DC on its network (tactical planning), and
3. Create weekly production line schedules for individual plants by product family (operational planning)

While the outputs and planning purposes of these three DSS models differed significantly, they also shared some common characteristics. Each model included production rates, capacities, and costs for production lines at individual plants. Thus, AO had to ensure that the cost and capacity data used for an existing plant in its "strategic" manufacturing and distribution network model was consistent with the data in its "operational level" production scheduling model for this same plant. Similarly, demand forecasts represented key inputs that drove AO's strategic and tactical planning models, as well as its operational scheduling models.[3] The strategic forecasts projected product family demand five years into the future, while the tactical forecasts typically covered the next 18 months. To facilitate consistent planning across all levels, AO planners had to assure there was alignment between the strategic and tactical forecasts, as well as the operational forecasts.

It may seem self-evident that a firm must assure that data such as production capacities and demand forecasts remain consistent and aligned across all DSS models at all planning levels. However, in practice, maintaining this alignment often represents a major challenge for a supply chain organization, particularly those of mid-size and larger firms. The following case study provides an example of how one firm addressed this challenge.

A Case Study of a Logistics Decision Support System

The case study of a logistics DSS presented in this section is originally based on an implementation that one of the authors led at Warner Lambert (WL) in the late 1990s. This system remained in place and was expanded during the early to mid-2000s after Pfizer Inc acquired WL.[4]

In June 2000, Pfizer Inc. and Warner-Lambert Company merged to form the new Pfizer Company, whose annual sales exceeded $30 billion at that time. The consumer sector of Pfizer consisted of a number of global operating units including a consumer healthcare division that supplied over-the-counter-drugs and health and beauty aids. In the United States, a single logistics organization warehoused and distributed all of the products of the consumer businesses, as well as those of the firm's pharmaceutical division. The DSS described herein was originally developed to support the premerger WL US network, and after the merger, Pfizer continued to employ this DSS to support the combined Pfizer/WL US logistics network.

The original WL–US distribution network was essentially a two-echelon distribution network. The first echelon consisted of two large distribution centers in Elk Grove, Illinois and Lititz, Pennsylvania, while the second included over 35 small third party pool distribution locations dispersed throughout the United States. The merged Pfizer consumer and pharmaceutical distribution network included all of these locations and three additional echelon-one distribution centers that comprised the old Pfizer pharmaceutical and consumer division network. WL distributed finished goods to its customers' receiving locations (warehouses) either directly from its two major distribution centers, or in shipments that flowed from a distribution center to a pool distributor and then to the customer. Large consumer product orders flowed as truckloads from Elk Grove or Lititz direct to the customer, while small orders typically traveled from the DC to the pool distributor to the customer. Most pharmaceutical orders were delivered by courier services.

Motivation for Developing the Decision Support System

A number of factors motivated the WL logistics organization to develop a DSS, including the increasing pressure the firm had received from its customers to provide superior supply chain and logistics services. Distribution services are more than delivering orders on time and safely to customers. To be considered a "preferred" vendor of a large retailer, a supplier must also monitor, maintain, and provide information on all key elements of the supply chain between itself and its customers. The supply chain information that requires continuous review and updating spans a broad spectrum of functional activities and processes. However, suppliers and customers focus on the key drivers of supply chain relationships using metrics such as order cycle time, on-time delivery, order and line item fill rates, and delivery overages, shortages and damages.[5] WL also recognized that it had to improve its ability to make informed, rapid decisions about logistics planning over the traditional hierarchical framework discussed in Chapter 3. Thus, WL wanted a planning system to address diverse problems and functions over this broad planning horizon.

The Decision Support System

The foundation of an effective modeling and DSS system is a comprehensive database that provides historical information (and ideally forecast information) on all major "transactional" logistics activities (for example, detailed shipment histories, sales, and freight costs). The database must also have appropriate summary fields and hierarchical relationships to facilitate its efficient use. Data elements needed to support DSSs include:

- Historical sales (shipments) by end item, by location, and by product family
- Transportation rates, costs, accessorials, duties, and shipments by origin–destination pair, by mode, by weight and by cube[6]
- Transit times by origin–destination pair, and by mode
- Inventory (actual and targets) in units and at cost, by end item/SKU, and by location
- Manufacturing rates and costs by production line, by plant, by end item and by product family
- Purchasing costs and terms, by vendor, by location, by end item and by product family
- Tax information, local content rules and intracompany transfer pricing for global/international models
- Accounts receivable, deduction claims, shortage and damage claims, by customer and by location
- Well-defined hierarchical product line structure with data available at any level of product aggregation

WL's information systems group developed and maintained databases which included many of these elements.

The logistics organization of WL utilized these corporate databases directly, and also established it own logistics data warehouse. Briefly, the logistics data warehouse received data feeds from the corporate data warehouses as well as from other sources more pertinent to just the logistics function (e.g., proof of delivery transactions from third party transport providers). Importantly, in constructing its data warehouse, the logistics planning team considered all of its planning and scheduling requirements from the daily operational to the long run strategic. The logistics data warehouse development process had several key objectives including:

1. Provide all the data that logistics planners regularly employ for all operational through strategic analytics,

2. Use clearly identified sources and definitions for all data fields, and

3. Clearly define the relationship between individual fields of data.

Briefly, through diligent adherence to these objectives, the WL logistics organization successfully established a foundation which facilitated consistency in the data inputs employed across all planning horizons. The logistics data warehouse became the *single data source* employed by logistics planning colleagues for all decision support analyses. We will now review selected key components of the WL/Pfizer supply chain DSS.

Individual Elements of the Strategic and Tactical DSS

WL's DSS contributed to many decisions concerning logistics, customer service, and the supply chain. However, its main purpose was supporting decisions regarding the US network for distributing finished goods including warehousing, transportation and customer delivery activities.

To support its long-run planning of warehouse capacities in the network, WL developed three linked simulation models: (1) a DC storage capacity model, (2) a DC picking and shipping model, and (3) a DC facility sizing model (Figure 4.4). Collectively these models evaluated the capacity

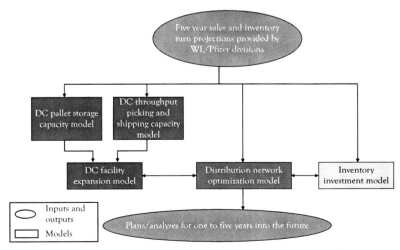

Figure 4.4. DSS components for strategic and tactical warehouse planning.

requirements and projections for the DCs on WL's network over planning horizons of two to five years, depending upon the decision in question. WL did its tactical and strategic planning of warehouse capacities as part of its overall integrated network planning. For example, in a typical strategic planning exercise, WL determined whether its warehouse network had sufficient capacity to handle its projected demands for the next 3–5 years.

The projected demand was based on a sales forecast consisting of a series of alternative forecast scenarios, each with a projected probability of occurrence. These alternative forecasts facilitated sensitivity analyses on the base case (the most likely scenario). Projections of finished goods inventory turns also drove the planning process. Because inventory turns play such an important role in determining total storage space requirements, WL also utilized alternative projections of turn rates in its sensitivity analyses.

The outputs of the individual planning models became inputs to the other models. In practice, the planning methodology was usually both sequential and iterative. First, planners input the sales and inventory projections for the planning horizon into the DC storage capacity and the DC picking and shipping capacity models. Each model projected the capacity utilization rates (surplus or deficit) over the planning horizon for its respective areas of warehouse operations. The outputs of these two models became inputs to the DC facility-sizing model. The DC facility-sizing model evaluated such factors as the total network-wide warehouse square footage required to store, pick, and ship the projected sales and inventory over the planning horizon.[7]

Projections for sales and finished goods inventory turns were also inputs to the distribution network optimization model. WL developed this optimization model of its US network as part of a project to evaluate long run warehouse capacity requirements. The optimization model was a mixed integer programming model that produced plans for the distribution of WL products over the planning horizon.[8] The model's results included projected product flows through the network by individual location, from plants to customers. It forecast the future product volumes that each warehouse would have to handle. In some applications, planners would run this model before running the DC pallet storage and throughput models to identify the projected portion of total demand each DC would handle. In other cases, a supply and distribution plan was in place, and planners would input the initial forecast for the planning horizon directly into the DC pallet storage and throughput models.

The inventory investment model shown in (Figure 4.4) represented the final major planning element in WL's strategic DSS. WL constructed several inventory models over the years including a traditional item level statistical safety stock model and several high level "portfolio effect" and "square root of N" models[9]. For most strategic applications, these models provided sufficient accuracy. WL planners typically integrated the inventory decision support models with the other models shown in Figure 4.4 using the iterative, scenario planning approach. Specifically, a series of strategic scenarios would be developed. These scenarios might propose alternative numbers of DCs for the network (e.g., 3 vs. 2) and alternative locations. For each scenario, the inventory model would project the overall level of inventory investment requirements on the network. This projection would then be disaggregated to the DC level. These projections would facilitate both a calculation of the total inventory investment and carrying cost of each scenario, as well as serve to validate the DC storage model projections for individual scenarios.

Over several years, the WL DSS system provided key inputs for a number of long-run distribution studies and decisions including:

1. the determination of whether WL should expand the first echelon of its two echelon network into a larger echelon (e.g., expand from two regional DCs to three regional DCs);
2. the determination of a new pharmaceutical transport delivery mode network; and
3. the determination of the best long-term US distribution network to serve the merged WL/Pfizer network (i.e., how to merge the old WL and the old Pfizer premerger networks).

Elements of the Operational DSS

At the operational level, WL developed a DSS that contained a toolkit of standardized reports, diagnostic models and analyses including the following:

- A customer logistics scorecard
- An order cycle monitoring tool
- An on-time delivery monitoring tool
- An inventory level and turns monitoring tool

- An overage, shortage, and damages monitoring tool
- A detention and delivery unload monitoring tool
- Daily alerts to transportation load planners on schedule improvement opportunities
- Daily alerts to planners on on-time delivery performance results
- Daily alerts to customers detailing any backorders that occurred

Also at this level, logistics analysts used the logistics planning toolkit, a customized "point-and-click" system, to monitor and analyze all key customer-related activities on the distribution network. One component of this toolkit was the customer logistics scorecard (Figure 4.5). Warner-Lambert maintained scorecards at the individual customer level, and additionally, by individual customer receiving location.

Illustrative customer logistics scoreboard

Customer	On-time delivery		Order cycle time		
	Actual	Goal	Mean	Std. Dev.	Goal
Customer 1	98%	97%	8.9	3.4	8.0
Customer 2	97%	97%	6.1	2.1	7.0
Customer 3	94%	97%	6.5	2.1	7.0
Customer 4	98%	97%	6.0	2.9	7.0

Customer	Line item fill rate		Order fill rate		Freight cost per pound	
	Avg.	Goal	Avg.	Goal	Actual	Goal
Customer 1	97.9%	98%	83%	85%	$0.024	$0.030
Customer 2	97.1%	96%	83%	82%	$0.027	$0.035
Customer 3	96.4%	97%	74%	80%	$0.036	$0.049
Customer 4	97.5%	98%	87%	79%	$0.031	$0.037

Customer	Percent of cases picked at DCs in full pallet and full layer quantities		Inventory turns	
	Actual	Goal	Actual	Goal
Customer 1	94.1%	90%	7	7
Customer 2	80.7%	85%	3	4
Customer 3	75.0%	70%	6	5
Customer 4	96.8%	99%	8	7

Customer	Carrier handling charges	Shortage claims	Carrier charges total	Total accesorials	Unearned cash discounts	Unsaleables
Customer 1	$10,000	$5,000	$9,000	$24,000	$50,000	$0
Customer 2	$2,000	$0	$2,000	$4,000	$70,000	$0
Customer 3	$10,000	$10,000	$4,000	$24,000	$0	$10,000
Customer 4	$7,000	$15,000	$7,000	$29,000	$0	$20,000

Figure 4.5. Illustrative components of operational DSS.

The WL/Pfizer logistics DSS continued to evolve and expand over time at the operational, tactical, and strategic levels. Specific analytic needs and projects often precipitated these ongoing enhancements. In this chapter we will discuss a major enhancement that was later developed to address daily inventory deployment decisions. We close our review of this DSS by noting that WL developed the initial major core elements of its logistics DSS in approximately two years. Over the next five plus years, the merged WL/Pfizer logistics organization relied heavily on this DSS, while continually enhancing and refining the individual components of the system.

Case Study: A Strategic and Tactical Global Manufacturing Planning DSS

In this section, we review a global manufacturing planning DSS implemented by a multibillion dollar confectionery manufacturer to support its strategic and tactical planning processes. This DSS relied heavily on mathematical optimization software. In recent decades, a variety of sophisticated mathematical optimization algorithms and heuristics have been implemented in commercial supply chain software. In many cases, users may not even be aware that mathematical optimization underlies the software that they are using, as it usually is not necessary to have technical knowledge of mathematical optimization to utilize commercial software based on these algorithms. This software ranges from operational production line scheduling and transportation vehicle routing applications to strategic large-scale manufacturing and distribution network rationalization applications.[10] For our purposes, technical details are not germane. Therefore, in the following case study, we will use a series of figures and accompanying text to illustrate a large scale optimization-based manufacturing planning implementation that the authors helped lead.

Case Study

The Adams division of WL and Pfizer (following the firms' merger) was a multibillion dollar manufacturer of gums and mints. The firm produced well-known products such as Dentyne, Trident, Chiclets, and Certs.[11] In the late 1990s, the Adams division wanted to enhance its strategic and tactical manufacturing planning capabilities, and so supply chain personnel decided to develop a global manufacturing and distribution planning model.

The Adams global manufacturing optimization model included all the major plants and products of the division. This represented over 12 plants scattered across the Americas, Europe, and Asia, and over 70 product families. Figure 4.6 illustrates where the Adams optimization model would fit in the hierarchical production and distribution planning framework described in Chapter 3.

Briefly, for tactical planning, the model could generate integrated production and sourcing plans for global manufacturing and distribution. As Figure 4.6 depicts, a solution to a planning run of the Adams optimization model generated:

- A global production plan for each production line of each plant, by product family, and
- A global sourcing plan indicating the plant to DC to country sourcing assignments and quantity flows by product family

For strategic planning, an enhanced version of the model could also evaluate decisions concerning plant location, closing, expansion, and contraction.

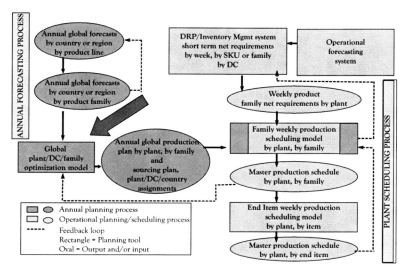

Figure 4.6. Integrated production and distribution planning system (tactical/annual planning and operational scheduling).

The Adams planning team began constructing the global network model by first identifying the capacities and costs associated with the three major production stages at its plants—bulk processing, finishing, and packaging. Then using commercial optimization modeling software, the team entered the manufacturing cost and capacity data. This process also required that the relationship between the different production stages be modeled explicitly (e.g., the number of bulk processing units required as input to produce a finished unit). Again commercial software renders tasks such as this easy for users to perform. On the logistics side, the planning team identified all pertinent warehouse costs and capacities, locations, echelons, as well as all appropriate transportation lanes, capacities, and costs. The planning team also input all of this data into its mathematical optimization software. Demand forecasts by product family, by country represented the driving constraint (requirement) that a solution to the integrated manufacturing and distribution optimization model had to satisfy. Thus, the team had to develop and implement these forecasts as part of the model-based planning process.

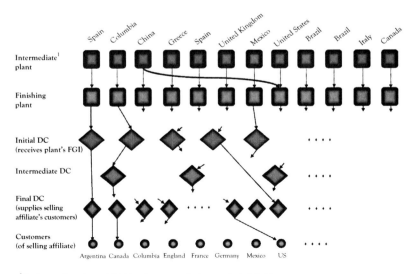

[1]The intermediate plant and finishing plant are actually the same physical plant in some cases

Figure 4.7. Schematic of network model.

Figure 4.7 displays an illustrative schematic of the manufacturing and distribution network imbedded in the optimization model. As shown, the manufacturing unit had two echelons, and product flows between the finishing plant and the destination country were in some cases direct, while in other cases could involve passing through several DCs.

Additional Background on the Optimization Model

To better understand the functionality and mechanics of the Adams DSS optimization model, consider Figure 4.8. This figure describes the key costs and constraints captured by the tactical planning version of the model. The model accounted for all major production and distribution costs, both fixed and variable. This included all relevant local country

---

COSTS

- **Production costs**
  - fixed (at the plant or line level)
  - variable (at the line and product family level)
- **Freight and duties**
  - inbound   – inter-facility   – outbound to customer
- Taxes
- **Distribution facility costs**
  - fixed
  - variable
- **Inventory carrying costs**

CONSTRAINTS

- Production capacities (at the line and product family level)
- Distribution storage and throughput capacities
- Inventory targets (by product family, location and time period)
- Demand forecasts (by product family, by country)
- Order cycle requirements, in days (for delivery to customers)

Figure 4.8. Key cost components and constraints in model.

taxes and duties on international flows. The strategic planning version of the Adams model also included:

- The one-time costs associated with opening new plants and DCs, and
- The one-time costs associated with closing existing plants and DCs.

The constraints displayed in Figure 4.8 represented a series of production and DC capacities, demand forecasts and inventory target levels, as well as customer delivery time requirements that a model planning solution had to satisfy. The constraints that drive a solution to an optimization model run are the demand forecasts that must be satisfied. Figure 4.9 offers an illustrative template of the demand constraint data the planning team would develop for a planning scenario. For tactical planning, the model might have anywhere from one time bucket (e.g., a 12-month period) to four to six buckets (e.g., 4–6 quarters in a 12–18 month planning horizon). For strategic scenarios, planners might again employ one or several time buckets (e.g., a five-year planning

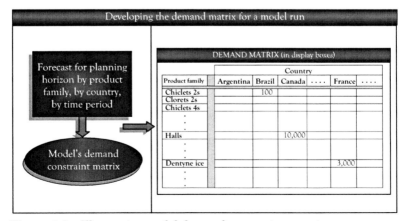

- The forecast by product family over the planning horizon drives the optimization model
- This demand constraint matrix allows the model to develop plans that minimize total network-wide delivered costs

Figure 4.9. Illustrative model demand constraint matrix.

horizon defined with annual buckets or a single period model evaluating an annual forecast five years in the future).

Figures 4.10 and 4.11 complete our illustration of selected model data inputs and constraints. Figure 4.10 depicts a three-stage gum and mint manufacturing process. Figure 4.11 describes the type of capacity data, by product family and production process that was developed for the Adams optimization model.

Figures 4.12 through 4.15 describe several illustrative model solution outputs to conclude this section.

Figure 4.12 shows the finished goods shipment quantities planned between each plant and destination country by product family. The actual model would produce a plan for each product family and in total. Figure 4.13 provides an example of the production plan by production line and product family generated for each plant. Figure 4.14 illustrates how the individual production and shipping plans for each plant and product family aggregate to global production and distribution plans. The two tables in Figure 4.14 highlight the powerful insights that the Adams' manufacturing and distribution optimization model generated. The solution algorithm of the DSS model simultaneously evaluated all the tens of thousands of individual costs, capacities, and other constraints such as

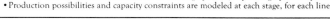

• Production is modeled as either a three- or two-stage process, depending upon the production process
• Production possibilities and capacity constraints are modeled at each stage, for each line

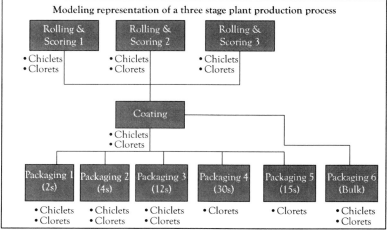

Figure 4.10. Illustration of how production is modeled.

Production capacity chart

Product family	Stage 1			Stage 2	Stage 3					
	Rolling & Scoring 1 (kg/hour)	Rolling & Scoring 2 (kg/hour)	Rolling & Scoring 3 (kg/hour) ①	Coating/ (kg/hour) ①	Packaging 1 (Display boxes/hr)	Packaging 2 (Display boxes/hr)	Packaging 3 (Display boxes/hr)	Packaging 4 (Display boxes/hr)	Packaging 5 (Display boxes/hr)	Packaging 6 (Display boxes/hr) ①
Chiclets 2s	1000	1000	2000	2000	500	–	–	–	–	–
Clorets 2s	1000	1000	2000	2000	500	–	–	–	–	–
Chiclets 4s	1200	1200	2000	2000	–	400	–	–	–	–
Clorets 4s	1200	1000	2000	2000	–	400	–	–	–	–
Chiclets 12s	1000	1000	2000	2000	–	–	600	–	–	–
Clorets 12s	1000	1000	2000	2000	–	–	600	–	–	–
Clorets 15s	1000	1000	2000	2000	–	–	–	500	–	–
Clorets 30s	1000	1000	2000	2000	–	–	–	–	700	–
Chiclets Bulk	1000	1000	2000	2000	–	–	–	–	–	1000
Clorets Bulk	1000	1000	2000	2000	–	–	–	–	–	1000

① The model will account for losses in yield between production stages

- The capacities stated in units per hour are translated into the actual time periods used in a model run. For example, if the model was evaluating an eighteen month planning horizon in quarterly periods, the above table would be translated into quarterly capacities

- Overtime is also modeled explicitly

Figure 4.11. Illustrative production capacity chart (for rolling and scoring lines at a plant).

Country	Projected Shipments Over Planning Horizon (000 cases) (Product Family = Halls)					
	Plant					
	Columbia	Brazil	Spain	China	United Kingdom	Canada
Argentina	1000					
Brazil	1000	500				
Columbia			500			
Canada		1000				
:	:	:	:	:	:	:
France						
:	:	:	:	:	:	:
Mexico						1000
:	:	:	:	:	:	:
US						1000

Figure 4.12. The model will produce a global sourcing plan by product family.

Production plan for plant ABC (recommended weeks of production over planning horizon)			
Product family	Line 1	Line 2	Line 3
Halls	30	52	0
Clorets	15	0	18
Certs	7	0	34
TOTAL	52	52	52

Figure 4.13. The model will also create a production plan by line for each plant.

Global Production Plan (cases - 000)						Global Distribution Plan (cases shipped - 000)					
	Plant						Plant				
Product family	Barcelona	Cali	....	Toronto	Total	Country	Barcelona	Cali	....	Toronto	Total
Certs						Argentina					
Dentyne						Brazil					
Dentyne Ice						Canada					
:						Chile					
Halls						:					
:						Mexico					
Trident						:					
:						Yugoslavia					
:						TOTAL					
TOTAL											

Figure 4.14. The model's individual (line and product family) production and distribution plans will aggregate to a recommended global production and distribution plan.

Illustrative Inventory Plan
(FGI in 000 cases at end of 1st period (e.g., quarter))

Product family	Brazil	Elk Grove US	Lititz US	Puebla	UK	. . .	Total
Certs							
Dentyne							
Dentyne Ice							
. . .							
Total							

DC[1]

[1]Plants can also have inventory targets in the model

Illustrative Inventory Plan
(FGI in 000 cases at end of 2nd period)

.
.
.

Illustrative Inventory Plan
(FGI in 000 cases at end of planning horizon)

Figure 4.15. The model will also produce a finished goods inventory plan by location for each subperiod in the planning horizon.

product family forecasts by customer, to create the "cost minimizing" integrated production and distribution plan for the entire network. Without the use of a mathematical optimization DSS tool, a planning team cannot develop a truly cost minimizing plan. It is simply too complex an undertaking without an optimization model. Figure 4.15 provides a template example of the finished goods inventory plan that an Adams modeling scenario would produce. For tactical planning purposes, projected inventory flows between periods represented a valuable planning output. However, for strategic scenarios where a planning team would evaluate such decisions as potential plant openings and closures, inter-period inventory flows would not represent an important consideration.

This completes our discussion of the Adams global manufacturing and distribution planning DSS model. This system provided numerous insights about the firm's global manufacturing network including the development of production product mix and technology plans that identified over $5 million in potential operational savings.[12] Strategic and tactical manufacturing–distribution optimization models can provide invaluable decision support to any firm with a moderate to large-scale network. This model certainly represented a key DSS component for the Adams division.

Case Study: An Operational Daily Inventory Deployment DSS

DSS that support short run operations vary widely from software and algorithms that schedule plant, warehouse, and transportation operations to dashboards that customer service personnel use to monitor supply chain services to customers. Despite the broad range of available commercial DSS tools, a supply chain organization cannot rely exclusively on turnkey tools to satisfy all of its DSS needs. To assure that its supply chain and logistics operations have the agility to react quickly to sudden, unforeseen operational challenges, a firm must also develop flexible internal DSS capabilities. In this section, we illustrate this need by reviewing a customized inventory deployment DSS that Pfizer developed to support daily logistics operations. As we now describe, the urgent need for this system arose quickly with minimal advance warning.

Case Study

In the early 2000s, following the merger of Warner-Lambert and Pfizer, significant storage capacity pressures suddenly began to impact the operations of the consumer distribution network. Specifically, the total pallets of finished goods inventory of the newly merged consumer division of Pfizer substantially exceeded the in-house pallet storage capacity of the consumer distribution network. The merger and several unanticipated internal issues created this rapid inventory buildup and capacity deficit. Both WL and old Pfizer had previously used third party overflow warehouse storage on an occasional, seasonal basis in the past. However, by 2001, it became clear that the newly merged firm would have to employ third party warehouse storage space as a standard component of its every day operating storage capacity. Neither a significant investment in internal storage capacity nor opening a new third party full service customer-facing DC, represented acceptable options. Thus, Pfizer logistics had to address its infrastructure capacity deficit with third party overflow warehouse storage. Throughput capacity, unlike storage capacity, did not represent an issue because the consumer DCs had ample throughout capacity.

To understand the potential complexity of managing the Pfizer consumer network with at times over 50 percent of finished goods inventory in outside overflow storage, consider Figure 4.16. This figure depicts the numerous different flows of finished goods into and out of the customer-facing distribution centers (Lititz and Elk Grove). As Figure 4.16 illustrates, finished goods produced at Pfizer plants and contract-manufacturing locations could potentially flow to copackers, to third party outside storage locations, or directly to the Pfizer DCs depending upon inventory requirements at any particular time.[13]

Inbound shipments to the Pfizer DCs could originate from Pfizer plants, Pfizer contract manufacturers, copackers, and third party outside storage locations. In total, inbound shipments to the DCs originated from well over 40 different locations. Finally, as Figure 4.16 depicts, the Pfizer DCs themselves often had to ship finished goods to copackers and to outside storage locations in addition to the DCs' shipments outbound to customers.

This potentially complex set of product flows is characteristic of consumer firms and industries. In particular, many consumer products firms utilize third party co-packers and contract manufacturing vendors to perform "kitting" type services. These third party vendors transform base finished goods products into promotional display items commonly found at grocery, drug, mass merchandiser, and other retail outlets. Thus, many manufacturers have a strong need for DSS that can guide daily

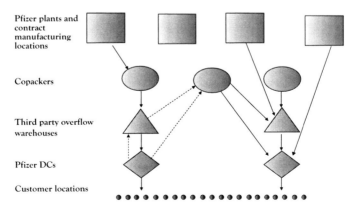

Figure 4.16. Potential finished goods product flows.

deployment operations that are more complex than the traditional "plant to manufacturer's DC to retailer's DC" flow. While traditional DSS tools such as DRP (distribution resource planning) systems can effectively provide decision support for the regular replenishment flows (e.g., of open stock base items), firms that manage the complex consumer products flows described herein often require additional DSS guidance.

To manage its complex set of product flows and inventory positioning decisions, the Pfizer logistics group determined that it required a DSS that would facilitate the effective daily deployment of inventory between all locations. This included daily inventory flows from:

- Outside storage locations to the DCs
- Plants, copackers, and contract manufacturing locations to the DCs
- Plants, copackers, and contract manufacturing locations to outside storage locations, and
- DCs to outside storage locations and copackers.

The complexity of managing daily inventory deployment decisions was particularly driven by the following business requirement. Pfizer's consumer customers required "single sourcing" for shipment deliveries. Specifically when a customer issued a purchase order (PO) for delivery of product, the customer required that all finished goods inventory items shipped to fulfill the PO originate from a single location and arrive on a single delivery. Thus, despite the fact that up to 50 percent of its total inventory might reside in outside storage, Pfizer logistics had to assure that it maintained sufficient inventory of all items in-house (i.e., in Lititz and Elk Grove) to facilitate "single-source, single delivery" order fulfillment.

The firm's ERP and warehouse management systems (WMS), although quite advanced, did not have sophisticated capabilities to deploy inventory between outside and inside storage locations. This is not surprising because typically ERP and WMS systems are designed to manage the flow and utilization of inventory within a warehouse. This capability (i.e., managing inventory within a warehouse) and the functionality required to manage associated activities such as warehouse trailer yard management represent more common ERP/WMS capabilities. Further, as previously noted, the logistics organization required not just the capability to direct inventory between inside and outside storage; but also it needed a system to direct whether inbound shipments from plants, contract manufacturers and copackers should flow to outside storage locations first, or directly into the Lititz and Elk Grove DCs. Thus, Pfizer logistics decided that it would have to construct a DSS to provide the functionality just described.

DSS Development Approach

Pfizer logistics already had an extensive DSS in place as described earlier in this chapter. Now to create a new operational DSS to guide daily decision-making on inventory deployment and warehouse operations, the logistics group leveraged the underlying data of this existing DSS. An informal team consisting of operations colleagues from the DCs and several colleagues from headquarters with business analytics and operations research backgrounds was formed. The team rapidly developed specifications for a series of daily reports that would help direct inventory deployment operations each morning. Specifically, the DSS had to provide guidance on all potential inventory deployment flows between all locations. This included all inventory item level flows involving plants, contract manufacturing locations, copackers, overflow warehouses, and the Pfizer DCs—a very extensive set of potential moves.

Data Flows to Support DSS

To address the additional data requirements for this new system, the development team decided to utilize the previously established links between the existing DSS systems and the firm's in-house ERP and warehouse management systems. Working with the IT organization, the logistics group had previously established processes and the necessary interfaces to facilitate nightly flows of files including the following data sets from corporate IT systems:

1. the current inventory positions of all items at all locations;
2. all orders for all items at all locations for as far into the future as they existed;

3. all forecasts for all items at all locations; and

4. shipment (i.e., sales) history for all locations for all items for the most recent 12 months.

These files and data sets, providing up-to-date information as of the close of business from the previous day, were received by a local server at the logistics headquarters and used to update a local logistics server and data warehouse. The logistics team determined what additional data fields it needed besides those already received in nightly flows from corporate IT. Because data feeds supporting the existing logistics DSS were already in place, it became a quick, easy task to append additional fields to these nightly flows, once logistics identified the newly required fields. Colleagues in the logistics group configured the DSS to automatically run a series of decision support analyses and reports each morning based on the updated data available on the logistics server.

Figure 4.17 lists many of the key analyses and reports created by the inventory deployment DSS.[14] The column in Figure 4.17 labeled "Description of Function" provides a brief overview of the role of each analysis and report. The purposes of the three "categories" of analyses and reports were:

a. to prioritize the unloading of inbound trucks transporting newly produced finished goods inventory (FGI) originating from plants, contract manufacturing locations and copackers;

b. to direct whether newly produced FGI originating from plants, contract manufacturing locations and copackers should be shipped to the DCs themselves or to the respective outside storage locations of the DCs; and

c. to deploy FGI between the DCs and their outside storage locations (i.e., to direct shipments from outside storage to the DCs and vice-versa, as well as any inter-DC transfers).

As described in Figure 4.17, the full set of morning reports collectively prioritized the unloading of inbound trucks at the DCs, directed the flow of newly produced FGI to either the DCs or their outside storage locations, and directed the flows of inventory between the outside storage

#	Report	Category	Description of function
1	Hot trailer list	A. Prioritize unloads	Prioritized order to unload inbound trailers that were in the DC's receiving yard
2	Divert or cold trailer list	A. Prioritize unloads	Identified any trailers in-transit to the DCs, and any inbound loaded trailers in the DC receiving yards which should be diverted to outside storage. This report served as a check to identify inbound trailers, if any, containing inventory that could be sent to outside storage but for some reason were routed direct to a DC
3	Plants to DCs inventory shipping report	B. Direct FGI to DC or outside storage	For each plant that replenished the DCs, directed which inventory items the plant should ship directly to each DC, and which items should be shipped to outside storage. (This daily direction was based on the inventory level of each item at each DC.)
4	Contract manufacturing plants to DCs inventory shipping report	B. Direct FGI to DC or outside storage	Provided the same daily shipping direction for contract manufacturing locations as report #3 did for Pfizer plants
5	Copacker to DCs inventory shipping report	B. Direct FGI to DC or outside storage	Provided the same daily shipping direction for copacker locations as Report #3 did for Pfizer plants
6	Outside to inside inventory shipping report	C. Deploy FGI within or from DC network	Identified inventory items and quantities that needed to be deployed from outside overflow storage locations to inside the DCs each day to fulfill customer orders and/or replenish DC inventory levels
7	Inside to outside inventory shipping report	C. Deploy FGI within or from DC network	Identified inventory items and quantities currently positioned inside the DCs that, if necessary, could be shipped to outside storage to open space within a DC for more critical inventory. For example, if item A had inventory significantly over the target level within a DC, and if item B had a dangerously low inventory level inside the DC; then a portion of A could be shipped to outside storage to make room for more inventory of B in the DC.
8	Outside storage to customer inventory shipping report	C. Deploy FGI within or from DC network	Identified "one-off" customer orders for a truckload quantity of a single item that could be shipped directly from outside storage to a customer. Occasionally a customer would place an order for a single item where the quantity ordered was a full truckload quantity. This report identified such orders so that the order could be shipped directly to the customer from outside storage.

Figure 4.17. Illustrative key daily DSS reports.

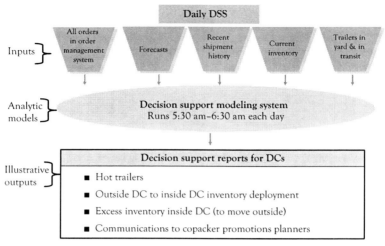

Figure 4.18. Methodology and algorithms of DSS.

locations of the DCs and the DCs themselves. Figure 4.18 offers an overview of the primary data flows and basic methodology of the system. The DSS received complete data updates every night from each key component of the customer order fulfillment IT supply chain; namely, the order management system (of the ERP), the warehouse and trailer yard management system, and the transportation scheduling system. These nightly data flows updated the DSS with the most current inventory positions of all items at all locations, all orders, and forecasts for all items at all locations; shipment history for all items at all locations; and in-transit and in-yard trailer information providing inventory information for all items on all trailers.

Summary

The Pfizer logistics organization implemented the initial version of this DSS quite rapidly, and the team began to use individual reports/analyses as soon as the first version of a planning analysis/report was constructed. A process quickly evolved whereby the team modified and enhanced individual analyses on a daily basis. The colleagues in operations would employ the updated DSS component for a day or two, and then request additional modifications based on learning's from using the DSS. Over time, each individual analysis of the DSS provided better, more precise day-to-day operational guidance. Similarly, the presentation formats of the analyses improved over time and offered clearer, easier to understand guidance for the logistics organization. Finally, often over a period of several weeks or months, individual DSS components reached their final analytic and presentation formats. Within approximately two to three months, the team had designed, developed, tested, and implemented the first full set of core algorithms and analyses. These initial core algorithms provided sufficient guidance to facilitate the effective use of overflow outside storage. Over the next year or so after the initial implementation, refinements, and enhancements to this DSS tool continued, and it was used for many years thereafter.

The rapid implementation of the inventory deployment system produced many short and longer term benefits. These included:

- The Logistics group had no administrative backorders during a period of several years where approximately 50% of its finished goods inventory was in outside storage. An "administrative" backorder was defined as a backorder resulting from inventory being positioned in outside storage when the inventory should have been positioned in a DC to fulfill an order.
- All inbound trailers to DCs were unloaded in a timely, efficient manner.
- Logistics had no administrative backorders where the inventory to fill an order was on a trailer that was in a DC inbound yard, but the DC had no inventory of the item(s) available within its four walls.
- Logistics maintained the appropriate balance of inventory between inside storage and outside storage at the SKU level.
- Incremental, avoidable extra shuttling of inventory between the DCs and their outside storage locations was minimized

The daily inventory deployment decision support of this system prevented an estimated $20 million dollars of potential revenue losses, and allowed Pfizer to maintain a high level of customer service. The ongoing commitment of the logistics organization to flexible, agile

DSS capabilities allowed it to respond quickly and effectively to a situation which could have significantly damaged its customer service levels.[15]

Conclusion: DSS Are Critical

The case studies in this chapter illustrate the need for a firm's supply chain organization to provide decision support for all levels of the planning hierarchy; the strategic, tactical, and operational levels. Further, when developing its DSS, a firm must assure that it maintains consistency and alignment between its data sources and inputs used at all three planning levels. For example, in this chapter, we observed the need for the Adams division to maintain consistent forecasts in its tactical and strategic manufacturing planning activities. The critical importance of a supply chain's commitment to DSS represented another key theme of this chapter. Support for DSS cannot be shortchanged. A supply chain organization must arm its colleagues with the data and analytic tools required to make good decisions and plans. Managers must also ensure that they have personnel who have the skill sets to exploit good DSS. Further, supply chain organizations must value and recognize colleagues with these skill sets. In closing, we emphasize again that the importance of a firm's commitment to DSS and colleagues who can effectively utilize these tools cannot be underestimated. Strong and effectively utilized supply chain DSS generate a competitive advantage for a firm.

CHAPTER 5

Frameworks for Supply Chain Performance Management

Introduction

The supply chain organizations of most moderate to large-sized firms are increasingly employing an array of dashboards, scorecards, key performance indicators (KPIs), and/or other measurement indices to monitor their performance. The development and availability of insightful metrics is a prerequisite for an effective performance management system. However, how a firm organizes its KPIs and how these KPIs align with its supply chain management decision framework and strategy represents an equally important issue. Thus, firms must not only have strong KPIs, but these KPIs must align seamlessly with the firm's supply chain management framework, activities, and strategy.

In this chapter, we present several frameworks that can enable a firm to synchronize its supply chain management plans and decisions with performance measures that monitor the impact of actions taken. We first introduce a hierarchical performance measurement system that provides a framework to house a firm's strategic, tactical and operational supply chain performance measures. We illustrate how this hierarchical performance measurement framework aligns with a firm's supply chain management activities at all three planning levels. We then present the supply chain operations reference (SCOR) model that provides another useful framework for identifying supply chain metrics and KPIs. SCOR is a hierarchical process reference model that is based on five level 1 supply chain processes that are decomposed into several nested levels. KPIs are associated with level 1 processes, while additional metrics are linked

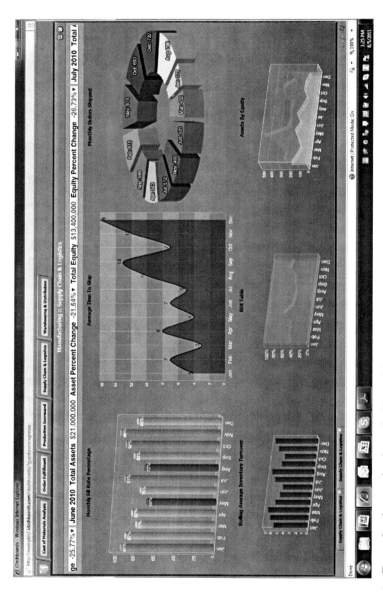

Figure 5.1. Example of a supply chain dashboard.[1]

to lower level processes. Drawing from both performance measurement frameworks we show how a set of KPIs can be linked to the firm's supply chain strategies as discussed in Chapter 2. These KPIs can be monitored using a scorecard or dashboard, as shown in Figure 5.1. Then we introduce an approach that transforms individual KPIs into a supply chain performance index that can monitor the overall impact of supply chain management plans and decisions over time.

A Hierarchical Framework for Performance Measurement[2]

Supply chain performance measures are needed for monitoring and control at three levels: strategic, tactical, and operational. In previous discussions of supply chain planning in this book (especially Chapters 2 and 3), these three levels were differentiated by their time horizon: long run, intermediate, and short run, respectively. In our supply chain performance measurement (SCPM) framework, the scale of an operation or activity that a particular performance measure monitors determines where it fits in the hierarchy. Within each of the three levels of the SCPM framework, we further differentiate performance measures as either external or internal. *External measures* focus upon the effectiveness of a firm's shipments or flows across a supply chain, while *internal measures* evaluate a firm's efficiency in producing its outputs and services. Typical external performance measures are order and line item fill rates on customer orders. For example, when a mass merchandiser places an order to a product supplier, these measures track whether the supplier delivers the total order and the individual items, respectively, on time and complete as ordered. However, these measures do not evaluate the supplier's order delivery cost, such as whether the order was delivered on time by expensive air freight rather than normal surface transportation. In this instance, the order delivery was effective, but it was not efficient. Internal performance measures such as "distribution cost per case" and "freight cost per pound" would be adversely affected by using the more expensive delivery mode.

Figure 5.2 displays the hierarchical SCPM framework, showing the three levels (strategic, tactical, operational), and the two measurement

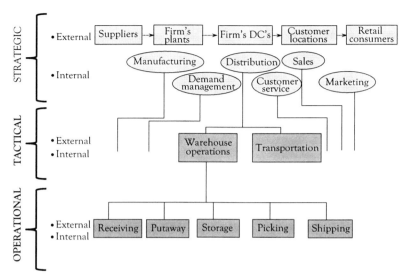

Figure 5.2. A hierarchical supply chain performance measurement framework.

perspectives (external and internal). At the strategic level from an external perspective, this framework spans the entire supply chain, from suppliers, through plants, distribution centers, customers, and consumers. From the internal perspective at the strategic level, we include the firm's top-level functions related to supply chain, such as distribution. At the tactical level, performance measures are required for such activities as warehouse operations and transportation, since these are the key functions of distribution. Drilling down into warehouse operations, we see from Figure 5.2 that it has five major subfunctions or processes at the operational level: receiving, putaway, storage, picking, and shipping. Internal and external performance measures are required at each level in this framework.

Figure 5.3 indicates how internal and external performance measures are set across the three levels of the SCPM hierarchy, continuing with distribution as our example. For the distribution organization (strategic level), percent of scheduled customer shipments delivered on-time, and the average and variance of order cycle lead time represent external measures, since they help to measure flows across the supply chain. They are strategic since they address the mission of the distribution function,

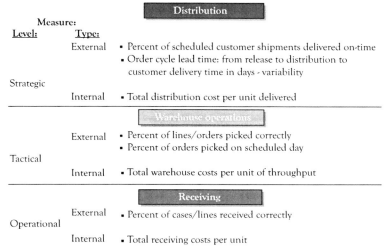

Figure 5.3. *Illustrative hierarchical performance measures for distribution function.*

ensuring delivery of products and services to customers in a timely manner. The total distribution cost per unit delivered is an internal, strategic measure since it measures the efficiency of distribution at the highest organization level.

At the tactical level, the percent of lines or orders picked correctly and the percent of orders picked on the scheduled day represent external measures because they evaluate the impact of warehouse operations across the supply chain. When a warehouse picks an order correctly, it contributes to the ultimate successful delivery of products to a customer who has placed an order. Similarly, when a warehouse picks an order on the scheduled day, this contributes toward a successful on-time delivery of products to a customer. The third tactical measure shown in Figure 5.3, total warehouse costs per unit of throughput, represents an internal measure, since it offers a summary view of the internal cost (and efficiency) of the warehouse operation.

Focusing on the warehouse receiving function at the operational level, the percent of cases (or lines) received correctly (i.e., accurately) is an example of an external performance measure. We categorize this measure as external because the accuracy with which this function

receives inbound shipments will impact the next stage of the supply chain. For example, suppose that the receiving area miscodes an
inbound receipt as product A, when in fact it received product B upon
delivery. If this error remains undetected, the shipment will then be put
into inventory classified as product B and at some future point could be
picked and delivered to a customer who ordered product A. Therefore,
the percent of lines or cases received correctly is classified as an external measure. In contrast, total receiving cost per unit has an internal
orientation and will be of most immediate concern to receiving and
warehouse personnel.

As another brief example consider manufacturing, which is slotted
at the strategic level in Figure 5.2. A major manufacturing function
such as fabrication would be at the tactical level, with fabrication subfunctions such as machining placed at the operational level (not shown
in Figure 5.2). Manufacturing cost/per unit would be an example of an
internal performance metric at the strategic level, processing cost/unit
would be an internal measure at the tactical level, while item defect rate
would be an external measure at the operational level.

The hierarchical SCPM framework offers a number of important
benefits. First, it provides a unified framework for aggregating performance measures across an organization. It enables a firm to organize its
key performance measurements into a structure that leads to a relatively
few, high level, strategic measures (e.g., between 10 and 25) that monitor overall firm performance. These are sometimes referred to as KPIs
or key performance indicators. Second, this structure facilitates having
additional performance measures that monitor smaller components of
a firm's operation that align with overall firm objectives. In this way
all functional areas can develop and maintain their own measures, and
contribute to an overall measurement system. In addition, each function can then focus on a few key measures to help improve its performance. Finally, the SCPM framework can contribute toward aligning
the collective activities of a firm to meet a desired mission and set of
objectives. For example, if a firm has a comprehensive measurement
system in place that covers its major functional areas, managers can view
the system in its entirety to identify any potential misaligned activities
or objectives.

The SCOR Model

The SCOR model offered by the Supply Chain Council[3] provides another useful framework for identifying supply chain metrics and KPIs. SCOR links supply chain processes, performance metrics, best practices, and people into a unified hierarchical framework. It was designed to support communication between supply chain partners and improve the effectiveness of supply chain management, and is based on five supply chain processes: Plan, Source, Make, Deliver, and Return, as shown in Table 5.1.

These processes constitute level 1 of the SCOR model, which describes the scope and top-level supply chain configuration. Level 2 processes differentiate the strategies of the level 1 processes. For example, *Make Level 2* processes include: make-to-stock, make-to-order, and engineer-to-order. Level 3 processes describe the steps performed to execute the level 2

Table 5.1. SCOR Management Processes[4]

SCOR process	Scope
Plan	The planning activities associated with operating a supply chain – gathering customer requirements, collecting information on available resources, balancing requirements and resources to determine capabilities and gaps, and identifying actions to close gaps
Source	The ordering (or scheduling) and receipt of goods and services – issuing purchase orders, scheduling deliveries, receiving, shipment validation and storage, and accepting supplier invoices
Make	The activities associated with the conversion of materials or creation of the content for services – materials conversion: assembly, chemical processing, maintenance, repair, overhaul, recycling, refurbishment, remanufacturing, and other conversion processes
Deliver	The activities associated with the creation, maintenance, and fulfillment of customer orders – receipt, validation, and creation of customer orders; scheduling delivery; pick, pack, and shipment; and invoicing
Return	The activities associated with the reverse flow of goods back from the customer – identification of need for a return, disposition decision making, scheduling the return, shipment and receipt of returned goods

processes. For example, *Make-to-Order Level* 3 processes include such activities as: schedule production activities, issue product, and produce and test. Finally, level 4 processes describe industry specific activities needed to execute level 3 processes. For example, *Issue Product Level 4* activities for the electronics industries include: print pick list, pick items, deliver bin to production cell, and so on. SCOR does not detail level 4 processes; these are developed by organizations and industries.

SCOR incorporates five supply chain performance attributes: reliability, responsiveness, agility, costs, and assets. The importance of these attributes is tied to the organization's strategy. Linking back to supply chain strategic planning discussed in Chapter 2, among our supply chain objectives were cost efficiency, delivery effectiveness, and flexibility, which are closely aligned with selected SCOR attributes. In Table 2.1, we provide a set of metrics that can indicate achievement of each of these objectives. Similarly, SCOR includes metrics to monitor the achievement of the five attributes at each level of the process hierarchy. At level 1, the measures are strategic and are KPIs. SCOR lists the processes that influence the performance of a level 1 KPI and the level 2 metrics that should be analyzed to identify the factors contributing to the current level of performance. By examining the level 2 metrics, managers can determine the level 3 processes and metrics that should be investigated.

Table 5.2 lists the SCOR KPIs and their definitions as they relate to each of the supply chain attributes. Interestingly, the KPIs associated with the first three attributes (reliability, responsiveness, and agility) are external and customer-focused, while the second two (costs and assets) are internally focused, supporting the need for a mix of internal and external KPIs, as previously discussed. We also note that a firm may wish to track selected level 2 metrics as well depending on their strategy. For example, inventory days of supply for finished goods, a level 2 metric under assets, may be a KPI for high-volume, consumer goods manufacturers.

SCOR offers a number of important advantages when applied to supply chain performance management. It provides a process-oriented framework for measuring and understanding the drivers of supply chain performance and creates a foundation for improvement. In addition, the SCOR metrics and KPIs are tied to specific performance attributes, allowing comparison across different supply chains and strategies.

Table 5.2. SCOR Level 1 KPIs by Attribute[5]

Supply chain attribute	KPIs
Reliability	Perfect Order Fulfillment – The percentage of orders meeting delivery performance with complete and accurate documentation and no delivery damage. Components include all items and quantities on-time using the customer's definition of on-time, and documentation—packing slips, bills of lading, invoices, etc. ([Total Perfect Orders]/[Total Number of Orders] × 100%)
Responsiveness	Order Fulfillment Cycle Time – The average actual cycle time consistently achieved to fulfill customer orders. For each individual order, this cycle time starts from the order receipt and ends with customer acceptance of the order ([Sum Actual Cycle Times For All Orders Delivered]/[Total Number Of Orders Delivered])
Agility	Upside Supply Chain Flexibility – The number of days required to achieve an unplanned sustainable 20% increase in quantities delivered. Upside Supply Chain Adaptability – The maximum sustainable percentage increase in quantity delivered that can be achieved in 30 days. Downside Supply Chain Adaptability – The reduction in quantities ordered sustainable at 30 days prior to delivery with no inventory or cost penalties. Overall Value at Risk – the sum of the probability of risk events times the monetary impact of the events which can impact any core supply chain function (e.g., Plan, Source, Make, Deliver and Return) or key dependencies.
Costs	Supply Chain Management Cost – The costs associated with operating the supply chain (Sales – Profits – Cost to Serve). Costs to serve include marketing, selling, and administrative costs. Cost of Goods Sold – The cost associated with buying raw materials and producing finished goods. ([direct material costs] + [direct labor costs] + [indirect costs related to production]).
Assets	Cash-to-Cash Cycle Time – The time it takes for an investment made to flow back into a company after it has been spent for raw materials ([Inventory Days of Supply] + [Days Sales Outstanding] – [Days Payable Outstanding]) Return on Supply Chain Fixed Assets the return an organization receives on its invested capital in supply chain fixed assets ([Supply Chain Revenue] – [COGS] – [Supply Chain Management Costs])/[Supply-Chain Fixed Assets]) Return on Working Capital – assesses the magnitude of investment relative to a company's working capital position versus the revenue generated from a supply chain [Supply Chain Revenue] – [COGS] – [Supply Chain Management Cost])/([Inventory] + [Accounts Receivable] – [Accounts Payable])

Linking Performance Management to Strategy

The frameworks for performance management previously presented differ in that the first hierarchical SCPM system has a functional and planning orientation, while SCOR is a process reference model. However, both highlight the need for internal and external KPI's that cover the various components of the supply chain and the importance of linking these measures to the firm's mission and strategy. Either of these frameworks can be applied in developing a set of performance measures and KPIs. A third approach is to link the selection of KPIs directly to supply chain strategy, and will now be discussed.

In Chapter 2 we showed how to align specific supply chain strategies with the mission through the achievement of objectives, and to select supply chain projects that will help achieve the strategies. Our challenge for performance management is similar, in that we wish to link the KPIs to the mission through the achievement of the supply chain strategies. Returning to our example of Zenith Corporation in Chapter 2, our approach is to modify Figure 2.2 and replace projects with KPIs, as shown in Figure 5.4. We begin by identifying a set of potential KPIs, and then from that broader set, select those KPIs that are best linked with the strategies. The selected set of KPIs will be monitored, and managerial interventions may be initiated to improve supply chain performance.

We begin by placing the level 1 SCOR KPIs defined in Table 5.2 in our set of potential KPIs. We should also consider including some level 2

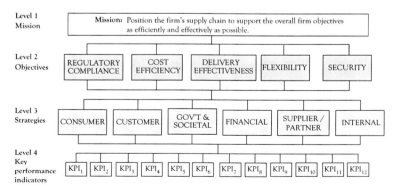

Figure 5.4. Linking KPIs to the supply chain mission, objectives, and strategies.

metrics from SCOR, and the types of measures discussed in the SCPM system. Each of the metrics identified would then be evaluated with respect to its achievement of the supply chain strategies, with those having the most impact included in the set of KPIs to be monitored and tracked. We note that a given metric may support one or more strategies. For example, perfect order fulfillment supports both the customer and consumer strategies. The customer strategy is directly supported since this KPI promotes great customer service, while the consumer strategy is indirectly supported, since this KPI will lead to improved product availability.

An illustrative set of KPIs that support the strategies shown in Figure 5.4 are given in Table 5.3. A firm using this approach in practice would substitute its KPIs for those shown in Table 5.3. In the "Strategies Supported" column, the strategy most directly supported by the KPI is listed first. The "Orientation" column indicates whether the KPI has an internal or external focus. The composition of KPIs in Table 5.3 includes four SCOR KPIs from Table 5.2 (nos. 1, 2, 5, 7), one modified

Table 5.3. KPIs Supporting Zenith's Strategies

No.	KPI	Strategies supported	Orientation (internal/external)
1	Perfect order fulfillment	Customer, Consumer	External
2	Order fulfillment cycle time	Customer, Consumer	External
3	Product availability on shelf	Consumer, Customer	External
4	Product satisfaction survey	Consumer, Customer	External
5	Upside SC flexibility	Customer, Consumer	External
6	Material recycled/material disposed	Gov't/Society	External
7	Cash-to-cash cycle time	Financial, Internal	Internal
8	SC management cost/$100k revenue	Financial, Internal	Internal
9	Inventory carrying cost/ inventory value	Financial, Internal	Internal
10	FTEs in SC planning/$1B revenue	Internal, Financial	Internal
11	On-time supplier delivery	Supplier/Partner	internal
12	Defects/100 supplier shipments	Supplier/Partner	Internal

SCOR KPI (no. 8), two financial/internal KPIs often monitored in practice (nos. 9, 10), and three KPIs needed to monitor the Govt/Society and
Supplier/Partner strategies (nos. 6, 11, 12). As shown in Table 5.3, it is
necessary to have at least one KPI tied to each strategy. The set of KPIs is
balanced to include an equal number of internal and external measures.
These KPIs can be incorporated into a supply chain dashboard or scorecard for ongoing monitoring of performance.

If the firm wishes to determine the relative importance of the KPIs,
they can be scored based on the extent to which they support the achievement of strategies. To illustrate this, recall in Chapter 2 that we introduced a simple scoring system to rate the relative importance of a set of
strategies in a mission, objective, and strategy (MOS) framework. Each
strategy was assigned points indicating its relative importance, and the
points of all six strategies had to total to 100.

Now returning to the scoring KPIs, assume that the Customer strategy has a score of 20 and the planning team believes that KPI1 (perfect
order fulfillment—from Table 5.3) very strongly supports this strategy.
Therefore, the planning team might elect to score KPI1 at the 95% level,
and so allocate it 19 (0.95*20) points. Since KPI1 indirectly supports the
Consumer strategy, its total score would be obtained by simply summing
the points earned from both the Customer and Consumer strategies. The
remaining strategies would be scored in a similar fashion.

Of course it is not absolutely necessary to use a scoring approach like
the one outlined above, but it is helpful in deciding how much emphasis
to place on the individual KPIs. In some instances, a firm may wish to
use a more formal process to weigh and score the KPIs. The Analytic
Hierarchy Process (AHP) mentioned in Chapter 2 and demonstrated in
the Appendix to Chapter 2 for evaluating and selecting projects, can be
applied for this purpose.[6]

Creating an Index to Monitor Supply Chain Performance

A supply chain performance index (SCPI) can be used to track the firm's
progress in achieving its strategies and carrying out its mission. The
advantage of creating a SCPI is that overall supply chain performance is

represented by a single aggregate measure. The SCPI is a weighted average of the points associated with all of the KPIs that comprise the index. The weights discussed in the previous section provide the relative importance of the KPIs in contributing to the SCPI. These weights can be developed through discussions with the supply chain planning and/or management team. Each KPI begins with 100 points and its points are adjusted from time period to period (e.g., quarter to quarter) based on the change in the value of its KPI. For our example, we will use the KPIs found in Table 5.3 to create an SCPI. An explanation of the process of determining the SCPI follows.

The first step is constructing a baseline value or score for the index in an initial or baseline period such as the first quarter of the year. The baseline value provides an index score against which we can then measure the value of the index in subsequent time periods. Table 5.4 illustrates the baseline index that is tied to the achievement of Zenith's supply chain strategy. The "Baseline Value" represents the actual value of the KPI during the initial time period. For example, 85% is the baseline value for perfect order fulfillment. To initiate the baseline index, each KPI is assigned 100 points. That is, an 85% value of perfect order fulfillment is linked to 100 points. To determine the baseline value of the SCPI we multiply each KPI's baseline points (100 in all cases) by its weight, and then sum the results. Note that by construction the baseline value of the SCPI is always 100, since the weights sum to 100%.

We can now compute the SCPI for the next quarter. For each KPI we must determine its percentage change (positive or negative) over the baseline and then multiply the result by the baseline points to determine the adjustment points required. The adjustment points are combined with the baseline points to determine the next quarter's points. The calculation is much simpler than it sounds. For example, from Table 5.4 we see that perfect order fulfillment increased from 85% to 87%. We determine its change over the baseline by using the formula: 100 * (New KPI value – Baseline KPI value)/Baseline KPI value, or 100 * (87% – 85%)/85%, or a 2.4% improvement. Therefore, the perfect order fulfillment points for next quarter are 100 + 2.4%*100, or 102.4. The same process can be used for all KPIs where an increase in value represents an improvement in performance (specifically, KPIs 1, 3, 4, 6, and 11). However, for the

Table 5.4. Example of a Supply Chain Performance Index

		Baseline quarter			Next quarter		
No	KPI definition	Value	Points	Weights	Value	Points	Weights
1	Perfect order fulfillment (%)	85%	100	0.14	87%	102.4	0.14
2	*Order fulfillment cycle time (days)*	5	100	0.11	4	120.0	0.11
3	Product availability on shelf (% days above min)	75%	100	0.08	70%	93.3	0.08
4	Product satisfaction survey (% satisfied)	80%	100	0.07	83%	103.8	0.07
5	*Upside SC flexibility (days)*	6	100	0.03	7	83.3	0.03
6	Material recycled/ material disposed (%)	15%	100	0.11	16%	106.7	0.11
7	*Cash-to-cash cycle time (days)*	30	100	0.12	31	96.7	0.12
8	*SC management cost/$100k revenue (%)*	10%	100	0.08	9%	110.0	0.08
9	*Inventory carrying cost/ inventory value (%)*	20%	100	0.05	22%	90.0	0.05
10	*FTEs in SC planning/$1B revenue (no.)*	35	100	0.06	33	105.7	0.06
11	On-time supplier delivery (%)	80%	100	0.07	85%	106.3	0.07
12	*Defects/100 supplier shipments (%)*	5%	100	0.08	4%	120.0	0.08
		Baseline Index 100.0			Performance Index 104.8		

Note: If a KPI definition is italicized, improved performance is indicated by a decrease in the KPI value.

remaining KPIs (indicated by italics in Table 5.4) our calculation process must change because a *decrease* in value is an improvement in performance. For example, KPI2, order fulfillment cycle time, improved from the baseline to the next quarter since it *dropped* from 5 to 4 days. We determine its change over the baseline by reversing the order of the two terms in the numerator of our formula: 100 * (Baseline KPI value − New KPI value)/Baseline KPI value. Therefore, KPI2 improved by 100*(5 − 4)/5, or 20% over the baseline, and so the points for the next quarter are 100 + 20%*100 = 120.

Once all of the KPI points for the next quarter are determined, we can compute the SCPI for the next quarter by multiplying the same weights used to compute the baseline index by the new points, and then summing the results. In our example as shown in Table 5.4, the overall change in performance was good, increasing from the baseline value of 100 to next quarter's index value of 104.8. This 4.8% increase indicates that the firm has made significant progress in executing its strategies. The individual KPIs comprising the SCPI can be examined to determine the main drivers to the changes (if any) in its value. Over time, the change and rate of change in such an index provides a quantitative perspective on overall progress.

Conclusion: Improving Performance

The frameworks that we have presented are designed to enable a firm to monitor and track its supply chain performance and to determine if their strategies are being successfully executed. Performance management can help to close the loop on the strategy formulation, implementation, and execution processes. If performance is not meeting expectations, the issues impeding performance must be uncovered and appropriate managerial actions taken. Alternatively, expectations could be altered, leading to possible changes in action plans and strategies.

Firms may wish to embed their KPIs and/or performance index into a scorecard or dashboard to simplify the monitoring process. Using business intelligence software, it is helpful to be able to "drill down" a KPI from the corporate level down to the product line or SKU level to better understand the drivers of performance.

CHAPTER 6

Conclusion

In this book we have reviewed a broad range of planning frameworks to facilitate effectively managing and monitoring a supply chain. We began in Chapter 1 with a general introduction to hierarchical planning frameworks, and a description of their applicability to supply chain planning and operations management. Chapter 2 explored the opportunity to employ methodologies such as the Mission, Objective, and Strategy (MOS) framework to enhance a firm's supply chain strategic planning process. This discussion introduced approaches for directly linking a firm's supply chain strategic project selection process to an MOS framework. We also reviewed straightforward project prioritization and weighting schemes, as well as the Analytic Hierarchy Process (AHP).

Chapter 3 commenced with further discussion of the rationale for utilizing "hierarchical planning frameworks" as a supply chain management tool. We then introduced a generic framework for hierarchical supply chain planning, and followed that with a case study of a strategic, tactical, and operational framework implementation by Pfizer. In this chapter, we also illustrated how a firm can apply a hierarchical planning process to each of its major individual supply chain functions such as manufacturing, procurement and transportation. These illustrations emphasized the importance of constructing planning frameworks that assure linkages and integration across all supply chain functions, as well as an ability to view and plan each function hierarchically. Chapter 4 highlighted that decision support systems and methods represent a critical component of supply chain management frameworks. To illustrate the value of DSS, we considered two case studies. The first case covered the implementation of a strategic and tactical global optimization model-based planning system by the Adams confectionery division of Warner-Lambert. For an "operational" DSS perspective, we reviewed a second case of a daily inventory deployment system developed and implemented by Pfizer. These cases both conveyed that effective supply chain planning requires both frameworks to organize the process, and an assortment of DSS tools to facilitate planning and scheduling activities.

Finally, Chapter 5 incorporated supply chain performance measurement frameworks into our arsenal of management tools. We reviewed two different hierarchical frameworks for organizing a firm's supply chain performance metrics. These included a strategic, tactical, operational hierarchy developed and implemented by the authors at Warner-Lambert, and the well-known SCOR model developed by the Supply Chain Council. Then we presented an approach that transforms individual KPIs into a supply chain performance index that can monitor the overall impact of supply chain management plans and decisions over time.

The supply chain planning and performance frameworks, and the complementary decision support systems and methods presented in this book can lead to better decision making from the strategic through the operational levels. The specific frameworks and DSS we have described provide a wide array, but by no means comprehensive, set of tools to facilitate improved supply chain planning and operations. To conclude this book, we now present some ideas on how interested practitioners may incorporate these frameworks and tools into their own supply chain planning and management processes.

How to Get Started—General Thoughts

Each firm must assess its own level of supply chain planning capabilities and decision support tools to decide how it can effectively use the approaches we have presented. For example, firms that believe their capabilities are relatively nascent may want to focus on planning at the strategic level so that they can identify high impact projects and initiatives which align with their objectives and strategies. These action plans can have the greatest impact on supply chain performance if they are successfully executed. Firms that have well established, mature supply chain planning capabilities should review their current frameworks and DSS across all levels. Questions to address in this review include:

1. *Does our supply chain organization have adequate DSS tools at all three planning levels?*
2. *Are our frameworks and the processes behind them clearly defined?*
3. *Are all of our major supply chain functions linked into our planning and scheduling frameworks? Or are there certain functions that are relatively isolated and need to be better integrated into our supply chain planning frameworks?*
4. *Do we have the appropriate levels of integration both between and within planning levels?*

These four questions illustrate the types of queries managers and executives of more mature supply chain organizations should ask themselves.

Regardless of the maturity and capabilities of a supply chain organization, there are at least three fundamental questions to evaluate that can direct a firm to its next steps, and to prioritize its initiatives. Specifically, we recommend that practitioners and executives ask the following three questions:

1. *Where are the greatest gaps in our current supply chain planning capabilities?*
2. *What initiative or initiatives will have the greatest immediate impact on our supply chain effectiveness and efficiency, if successfully executed?*
3. *What initiative or initiatives will have the greatest long run impact (or "multiplier effect"), if successfully implemented?*

We have found that these three questions are extremely pertinent regardless of where on the supply chain planning capability spectrum a firm may be. The third question (what initiative will have the greatest long run impact or multiplier effect) requires further explanation. Some projects or initiatives, if successfully implemented, spawn the development and implementation of related projects and initiatives in a supply chain organization. Other projects or initiatives may have a more one-time or stand-alone impact. That is to say, the successful implementation of this latter type of initiative does not trigger other substantive, beneficial initiatives. Projects or initiatives that lead to the development and implementation of secondary projects can be described as having a "multiplier" effect on an organization. Projects and initiatives that don't stimulate these related secondary efforts can be described as having "minimal" multiplier effects. Our experience in implementing frameworks and DSS tools indicates that projects with significant multiplier effects generally have the greatest long run benefit for a supply chain organization.

To illustrate the guidance that asking questions such as where are the greatest gaps, what initiatives will have the greatest immediate impact, and what initiatives will have the greatest long run, multiplier effects: consider the following example.

Example of Framework and DSS Implementation that Filled a Gap and Spawned Multiplier Effects

Recall in Chapter 3 that we reviewed the hierarchical supply chain planning framework implementation of American Olean (AO) Tile Company. This case offers a good example of how evaluating certain key questions can yield valuable direction on how to get started, or to identify the next steps in the supply chain framework and DSS development process. Figure 6.1

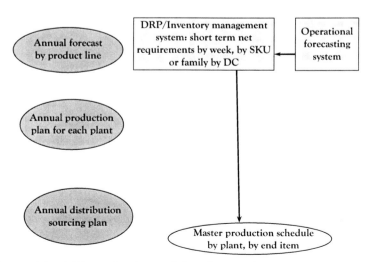

Figure 6.1. AO's production and distribution planning system: pre-HSCP implementation.

displays AO's pre-HSCP tactical (annual) and operational planning and scheduling decision support system.

The firm's annual planning basically consisted of three independent activities: (1) the development of high-level, divisional product line forecasts by the marketing department, (2) the development of a plant-level production plan for each plant by the manufacturing department, and (3) the development of a distribution sourcing plan by the distribution department. These three activities were not integrated (e.g., the manufacturing plan was not driven by the annual marketing forecast) and were primarily manual exercises. Any "cost-based" decisions in the manufacturing or distribution planning activities considered only the costs of the individual respective functional area. The primary components of AO's operational planning and scheduling system (before its HSCP implementation) consisted of: (1) an inventory management system which the firm used to manage its distribution network, and (2) end item master production scheduling activities which occurred at each plant. To summarize briefly, AO had some elements of an integrated system in place prior to its HSCP implementation. However, it also had a number of significant planning "gaps and disconnects", particularly at the annual planning level. Finally, minimal links, if any, existed between the annual and operational planning and scheduling levels.

After reviewing its entire manufacturing and distribution planning system, AO identified that its most significant planning gap existed at the tactical (annual) level between its production and distribution planning processes. The firm concluded that if it could develop a methodology and DSS tool to integrate these two planning activities, this would have the most beneficial impact on its supply chain of any potential initiative. At the operational level, AO's plants already had good master scheduling capabilities, and its inventory planners had a strong inventory management system to plan distribution center and store inventories. However, at the next level up, the tactical level, there existed neither DSS tools, nor an integrated process.

AO decided that it would develop a mathematical optimization model-based tactical planning system which would simultaneously generate both annual production and distribution plans. AO's decision to initiate this project resulted from its assessment that this project would:

1. address the biggest gap in its supply chain planning process;
2. have the greatest immediate impact on the organization once implemented; and
3. would have the greatest long run "multiplier" impact on its supply chain.

Regarding the multiplier impact, AO recognized that the successful implementation of an optimization-model-based tactical planning system would ultimately require the implementation of other highly beneficial DSS tools and processes. For example, integrated production and distribution planning optimization models require product family forecasts (i.e., aggregate forecasts for similar individual end items produced on the same production lines) at the sales territory (customer region) level. As Figure 6.1 depicts, AO realized that it only generated high-level tactical forecasts by major product line and detailed end item forecasts at the DC operational level. Thus, AO did not have a forecasting process that linked its high-level tactical forecasts with its short run operational forecasts. There was no alignment or integration between these two independent forecasts. AO's managers understood its new optimization-model-based process would necessitate the development and implementation of related inputs such as an intermediate product family forecasting system. Hence, AO believed that its initial project, development of the optimization model, would stimulate and highlight the need for related beneficial projects such as the product family forecasting system.

Figure 6.2 displays the completed AO hierarchical supply chain production and distribution planning system with the additional forecasting models and scheduling processes implemented.

We previously discussed this system in Chapter 3; and therefore, will not discuss it further here. However, a comparison of Figures 6.1 and 6.2 illustrates the "multiplier" impact that AO's initial optimization model-based production and distribution planning project had on the firm's long run supply chain planning capabilities. This initial project (the

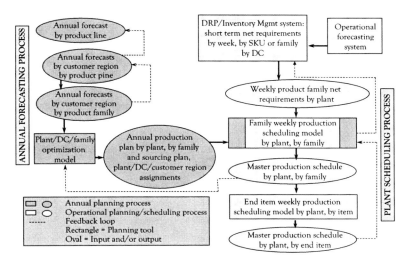

Figure 6.2. AO's hierarchical supply chain planning framework (tactical/annual planning and operational scheduling).

plant/DC/family optimization model) over a period of several years triggered the successful implementation of the comprehensive planning system shown in Figure 6.2.

Final Thoughts

There is no one right way to prioritize the development, enhancement, or fine-tuning of a firm's supply chain planning frameworks, DSSs and performance metric frameworks. However, we have found that answering questions such as: where are the greatest gaps, what initiatives will have the greatest immediate impact, and what projects will have the most beneficial long run multiplier effects—do provide strong guidance. Thus, we recommend asking and answering these questions about your organization's supply chain planning capabilities.

In conclusion, what is absolutely clear is that supply chain planning frameworks, DSS tools and performance metric systems are essential to facilitate supply chain operations excellence. These represent critical management tools that a firm must heavily invest in.

Notes

Chapter 1

1. Saaty (1996).
2. Chapter 5 will discuss SCOR. After reading Chapter 5, the reader can also find an overview of SCOR by reviewing "Supply Chain Operations Reference Model—Overview," Version 10.0 http://supply-chain.org/f/SCOR-Overview-Web.pdf Accessed July 29, 2011.
3. Anthony (1965).
4. Ackoff (1970).
5. Some of the material presented in this section was originally published in Miller (2002), and is reprinted with the kind permission of Springer Science + Business Media.

Chapter 2

1. Fisher (1997).
2. Lee (2002).
3. Bowersox and Daugherty (1987).
4. Autry, Zacharia, and Lamb (2008).
5. McGinnis, Kohn, and Spillan (2010).
6. We note that other business planning approaches can be applied to supply chain planning, including Strengths, Weaknesses, Opportunities, and Threats (SWOT) analysis: http://www.businessballs.com/swotanalysisfree-template.htm. This site provides an explanation of SWOT and templates for its application. Other approaches are Porter's Five Forces (Porter 2008) and the Resource-Based View of the Firm (Wernerfelt 1984).
7. Portions of the remaining sections of this chapter draw from Miller and Liberatore (2011).
8. For more on the MOS approach, see Liberatore, Monahan, and Stout (1992).
9. The journals reviewed included *Supply Chain Management Review, Logistics Management, Modern Materials Handling, American Shipper, DC Velocity, Global Logistics & Supply Chain Strategies, Interfaces, Outsourced Logistics, and Journal of Business Logistics.*
10. Autry et al. (2008)
11. Saaty (1996).

12. The authors have successfully utilized this method in practice several times; see e.g., Liberatore and Miller (1998).

13. The interested reader is referred to Saaty (1996) and Vaidya and Kumar (2006) as good starting points for addition background on the AHP methodology and its application.

14. Decision Lens Suite (2012) enables the user to quickly and easily structure hierarchies, enter the necessary judgments, and automatically compute the various weights. The consistency of each set of judgments is measured, and it provides the user with assistance in identifying the most inconsistent judgments.

15. Note that it is not required that the same weights be used for each individual rating scale for each criterion. Additionally, note that the weights on the rating scales are absolute, and do not need to sum to 1.0 (i.e., the supply chain planning team can establish whatever rating scale they feel is appropriate to "weigh" excellent, very good and so on).

16. A specific form of mathematical programming, called integer programming, is applied to make the project funding decisions; see Liberatore (1987) for further discussion.

Chapter 3

1. Some of the material presented in this chapter was originally published in Miller (2002), and is reprinted with the kind permission of Springer Science + Business Media.

2. American Olean is now part of Dal-Tile Company.

3. See Gupta, Peters, Miller, and Blyden (2002).

4. Miller (2002).

5. Exponential smoothing is a short range forecasting technique that forecasts next period's demand using the current period's forecast adjusted by a portion of this period's forecasting error.

6. See Miller (2002).

7. Linear programming is a mathematical technique that either maximizes or minimizes a linear function (an objective function) subject to satisfying defined linear constraints. For example, a production scheduling problem to be solved by a linear programming model would typically have an objective function "to create a production schedule that minimizes production costs" subject to satisfying the forecast "demand" constraints and "production capacity" constraints defined for the problem. Mixed integer programming is a related mathematical technique that can solve more complicated problems such as whether or not to open or close facilities on a network (i.e., what are termed 0–1 type decisions).

8.   Hax and Meal (1975).

9.   The reader familiar with the S&OP (Sales and Operations Planning) Process may recognize that a number of the forecasting, inventory management and capacity planning tools described in the AO Tile hierarchical planning system are also the types of tools often used by functions such as demand management, logistics and manufacturing to develop inputs and outputs for a firm's monthly S&OP process. Although hierarchical manufacturing and distribution planning frameworks and systems are not typically developed just to support an S&OP process, the components of these frameworks often can be leveraged for multiple purposes including S&OP support.

10. See Miller (2002).

11. Some of the material presented in this appendix was originally published in Miller (2009), and is reprinted with the kind permission of Springer Science + Business Media

12. See Miller (2002).

Chapter 4

1.   The reader interested in detailed descriptions of DSS is referred to a textbook on this subject by Liberatore and Nydick (2003).

2.   APICS (The Association for Operations Management, formerly known as the American Production and Inventory Control Society) defines distribution requirements planning (DRP) as "the function of determining the needs to replace inventory at branch warehouses". APICS defines master production scheduling (MPS) as "the anticipated build schedule for those items assigned to the master scheduler." Source: *APICS Dictionary 7th edition*, APICS Educational and Research Foundation, Annandale, VA, 1992.

3.   At the operational level, a combination of actual orders as well as forecasts was employed.

4.   Readers interested in the full case study are referred to Gupta, Peters, Miller and Blyden (2002) for a complete case description.

5.   Further discussion of the importance of supply chain metrics will be presented in Chapter 5.

6.   Accessorials are surcharges charged to shippers by carriers for additional services such as the driver assisting with unloading a delivery at the receiving customer's location (i.e., charges in addition to the basic fee charged for the transportation move).

7.   See Gupta et al. (2002) for additional information on the DC facility-sizing model.

8. A mixed integer programming model is an optimization model used to obtain a planning solution that either minimizes or maximizes a defined objective (e.g., minimize costs or maximize profits), while also satisfying a set of defined constraints (e.g., forecast demand requirements and production capacity limitations).

9. For background on these models see e.g., Maister (1976); Evers and Beier (1993); Tallon (1993); Tyagi and Das (1998); and Zinn et al. (1989).

10. The reader interested in detailed discussions and technical background on the use of optimization techniques to support supply chain and logistics operations is referred to Miller (2002) and Shapiro (2000).

11. The Adams business was sold by Pfizer to Cadbury in the early 2000s, and most recently, Kraft Inc acquired Cadbury.

12. See Gupta et al. (2002) for additional details on the benefits of this implementation.

13. Copackers are third party vendors that employ manual "kitting" type operations to create display pallets and promotional finished goods such as "on-packs". An on-pack is a promotional item where one finished good unit (e.g., a unit of toothpaste) is attached to another finished good unit (e.g., a bottle of Listerine) to create a new promotional unit.

14. Although the reports shown are illustrative and not the actual DSS reports, they do accurately depict the type of information conveyed by these reports.

15. Readers interested in additional details on the algorithms developed, the analyses created, and the reporting formats are referred to Miller (2012).

Chapter 5

1. Screen shot from http://examples2.idashboards.com/idashboards/?guestuser=wpman&dashID=55

2. This section draws upon concepts originally introduced in Miller (2002)

3. For an overview of SCOR, see http://supply-chain.org/f/SCOR-Overview-Web.pdf

4. This table is based on material found in: http://supply-chain.org/f/SCOR-Overview-Web.pdf

5. This table is based on material found in: http://supply-chain.org/metric/CO.1.2/en

6. See Saaty (1996). When using the AHP, all of the KPIs supporting a particular strategy would be pairwise-compared to determine their scores, as described in the Appendix to Chapter 2.

References

Ackoff, R. L. (1970). *A concept of corporate planning*. New York, NY: Wiley Interscience.

Anthony, R. N. (1965). *Planning and control systems: A framework for analysis*. Boston, MA: Harvard University Press.

APICS Dictionary. (1992). (7th ed.). Annandale, VA: APICS Educational and Research Foundation.

Autry, C. W., Zacharia, Z.G., & Lamb, C. W. (2008). A logistics strategy taxonomy. *Journal of Business Logistics 29*(2), 27–51.

Bowersox, D. J., & Daugherty, P. J. (1987). Emerging patterns of logistical organization. *Journal of Business Logistics 8*(1), 46–60.

Businessballs.com. (2012). *SWOT analysis*. Retrieved June 4, 2012, from business balls.com: http://www.businessballs.com/swotanalysisfreetemplate.htm

Decision Lens Suite. (2012). *Decision lens*. Retrieved December 31, 2011, from DecisionLens: http://decisionlens.com

Evers, P., & Beier, F. J. (1993). The portfolio effect and multiple consolidation points: A critical assessment of the square root law. *Journal of Business Logistics 14*(2), 109–125.

Fisher, M. L. (1997). What is the right supply chain for your product. *Harvard Business Review 75*(2), 105–116.

Gupta,V., Peters, E., Miller, T., & Blyden, K. (2002). Implementing a distribution-network decision-support system at Pfizer/Warner-Lambert. *Interfaces 32*(4), 28–45.

Hax, A., & Meal, H. (1975). Hierarchical integration of production planning and scheduling. In M. A. Geisler (Ed.), *TIMS studies in management science, Vol. 1, Logistics* (pp. 53–69). Amsterdam: North-Holland.

iDashboards Previews. (2011). *Supply chain & logistics*. Retrieved December 31, 2011, from iDashboards 7.5 a: http://examples2.idashboards.com/idashboar ds/?guestuser=wpman&dashID=55

Lee, H. L. (2002). Aligning supply chain strategies with product uncertainties. *California Management Review 44*(3), 105–119.

Liberatore, M. (1987). An extension of the analytic hierarchy process for industrial r&d project selection and resource allocation. *IEEE Transactions on Engineering Management 34*(1), 12–18.

Liberatore, M. J., & Miller, T. (1998). A framework for integrating activity-based costing and the balanced scorecard into the logistics strategy development and monitoring process. *Journal of Business Logistics 2*(2), 131–154.

Liberatore, M. J., & Miller, T. (1998). A framework for integrating activity-based costing and the balanced scorecard into the logistics strategy development and monitoring process. *Journal of Business Logistics 2*(2), 131–154.

Liberatore, M. J., Monahan, T. F., & Stout, D. E. (1992). A framework for integrating capital budgeting analysis with strategy. *Engineering Economist 38*(1), 31–43.

Liberatore, M., & Nydick, R. (2003). *Decision technology: modeling, software, and applications.* New York: John Wiley & Sons.

Maister, D. H. (1976). Centralization of inventories and the square root law. *International Journal of Physical Distribution 6*(3), 124–134.

McGinnis, M. A., Kohn, J. W., & Spillan, J. E. (2010). A longitudinal study of logistics strategy: 1990–2008. *Journal of Business Logistics 31*(1), 217–235.

Miller, T. (2002). *Hierarchical operations and supply chain management.* London: Springer-Verlag Press.

Miller, T. (2008). A hierarchical framework for supply chain performance measurement. *Future Pharmaceuticals,* online feature, August Day, 2008.

Miller, T. (2009). Notes on using optimization and dss techniques to support supply chain and logistics operations. In W. Chaovalitwongse, K. C. Furman & P. M. Paralos (Eds.), *Optimization and logistics challenges in the enterprise* (pp. 191–210). New York: Springer.

Miller, T., Peters, E., Bode, O., & Gupta, V. (2012). A logistics deployment system at pfizer. *Operations Research,* forthcoming.

Miller, T., & Liberatore, M. J. (2011). A practical framework for supply chain planning. *Supply Chain Management Review 15*(2), 38–44.

Porter, M. E. (2008). The five competitive forces that shape strategy. *Harvard Business Review 86*(1), 86–104.

Saaty, T. L. (1996). *The analytic hierarchy process.* Pittsburgh, PA: RWS Publications.

Shapiro, J. (2006). *Modeling the supply chain* (2nd ed.). Florence, K.Y.: South-Western College Publications.

Supply Chain Council. (2010). *Supply Chain Operations Reference (SCOR) model overview—version 10.0.* Retrieved December 31, 2011, from Supply Chain Council: http://supply-chain.org/f/SCOR-Overview-Web.pdf

Supply Chain Council. (2011). *Metric quick reference.* Retrieved December 31, 2011, from Supply Chain Council: http://supply-chain.org/metric/CO.1.2/en

Tallon, W. J. (1993). The impact of inventory centralization on aggregate safety stock: The variable supply lead time case. *Journal of Business Logistics 14*(1), 185–203.

Tyagi, R., & Das, C. (1998). Extension of the square root law for safety stock to demands with unequal variances. *Journal of Business Logistics 19*(2), 197–204.

Vaidya, O. S., & Kumar, S. (2006). Analytic hierarchy process: an overview of applications. *European Journal of Operational Research 169*(1), 1–29.

Wernerfelt, B. (1984). A resource-based view of the firm. *Strategic Management Journal 5*(2), 171–180.

Zinn, W., Levy, M., & Bowersox, D. J. (1989). Measuring the effect of inventory centralization/decentralization on aggregate safety stock: The square root law revisited. *Journal of Business Logistics 10*(1), 1–14.

Index

Announcing the Business Expert Press Digital Library

Concise E-books Business Students Need for Classroom and Research

This book can also be purchased in an e-book collection by your library as

- a one-time purchase,
- that is owned forever,
- allows for simultaneous readers,
- has no restrictions on printing, and
- can be downloaded as PDFs from within the library community.

Our digital library collections are a great solution to beat the rising cost of textbooks. e-books can be loaded into their course management systems or onto student's e-book readers.

The **Business Expert Press** digital libraries are very affordable, with no obligation to buy in future years. For more information, please visit **www.businessexpertpress.com/librarians**. To set up a trial in the United States, please contact **Adam Chesler** at *adam.chesler@businessexpertpress .com* for all other regions, contact **Nicole Lee** at *nicole.lee@igroupnet.com.*

OTHER TITLES IN OUR SUPPLY AND OPERATIONS MANAGEMENT COLLECTION

Collection Editor: M. Johnny Rungtusanatham

- *Production Line Efficiency: A Comprehensive Guide for Managers* by Sabry Shaaban and Sarah Hudson
- *Supply Chain Management and the Impact of Globalization* by James A. Pope
- *Orchestrating Supply Chain Opportunities: Achieving Stretch Goals Efficiently* by Ananth Iyer and Alex Zelikovsky
- *Transforming US Army Supply Chains: Strategies for Management Innovation* by Greg H. Parlier
- *Challenges in Supply Chain Planning: The Right Product in the Right Place at the Right Time* by Gerald Feigin
- *Lean Management* by Gene Fliedner
- *Design, Analysis and Optimization of Supply Chains: A System Dynamics Approach* by William R. Killingsworth
- *Managing Price Volatility: A Supply Chain Perspective* by George A. Zsidisin and Janet L. Hartley
- *Improving Business Processes Using Lean* by James R. Bradley
- *Cost Modeling for the Operations and Supply Chain Professional* by Victor E. Sower and Christopher H. Sower

- *RFID for the Operations and Supply Chain Professional* by Pamela Zelbst and Victor E. Sower
- *Global Supply Chain Management* by Matt Drake
- *Quality Beyond Continuous Incremental Improvement* by Victor E. Sower and Frank Fair

CPSIA information can be obtained at www.ICGtesting.com
Printed in the USA
BVOW020726161012

303120BV00007B/1/P

9 781606 493168